GCSE WJEC English
Reading Non-Fiction Texts
The Study Guide

This book is for anyone doing **GCSE WJEC English** or **GCSE WJEC English Language** at foundation level.

It's a **step-by-step guide** to becoming an expert on the Unit 1: Reading: Non-Fiction Texts exam.

It's got **everything you need** — an exam-focused guide to analysing the texts, a sample exam and worked answers to help you get **the grade you want**.

It's ideal for use as a classroom study book or a revision guide.

What CGP is all about

Our sole aim here at CGP is to produce the highest quality books — carefully written, immaculately presented and dangerously close to being funny.

Then we work our socks off to get them out to you — at the cheapest possible prices.

CONTENTS

Section Four — Writing Techniques

Section Five — Exam Techniques

Section Six — The Exam

Section Seven — Sample Answers

Published by CGP

Editors:
Joe Brazier
Taissa Csáky
Charley Darbishire
Rachael Powers
Caley Simpson
Jennifer Underwood

Produced With:
Emma Aubrey

Contributors:
Caroline Bagshaw
Samantha Bensted
Lorraine Campbell
Graham Fletcher
Jane Harrison
Nicola Woodfin

ISBN: 978 1 84762 105 4

With thanks to Heather Gregson, Kathryn Mawson and Julia Murphy for the proofreading.
With thanks to Laura Stoney for the copyright research.

The Publisher would like to thank the following copyright holders for permission to reproduce texts and images:

With thanks to iStockphoto.com for permission to reproduce the photographs used on page 36.

Groovy website: www.cgpbooks.co.uk
Jolly bits of clipart from CorelDRAW®
Printed by Elanders Ltd, Newcastle upon Tyne.

Based on the classic CGP style created by Richard Parsons.

Photocopying — it's dull, grey and sometimes a bit naughty. Luckily, it's dead cheap, easy and quick to order more copies of this book from CGP — just call us on 0870 750 1242. Phew!

Non-Fiction Texts

This book will help you do better in your <u>Unit 1 exam</u> for <u>GCSE English</u> or <u>GCSE English Language</u>. This exam is on "Reading non-fiction texts".*

You need to show these Skills in the Exam

To do well in this exam, you need to be able to do these <u>important things</u>:

1) <u>Understand</u> what a text is <u>telling you</u> and use good <u>examples</u> from the text to back up your points. You'll also have to <u>compare</u> texts (say how they're similar and how they're different) and use <u>examples</u> to back up your points.

2) <u>Work out</u>, and <u>explain clearly</u>, what the writer's <u>ideas</u> are and what their <u>point of view</u> is.

3) Explain how writers use <u>language</u>, <u>grammar</u>, <u>layout</u> and <u>structure</u> to make their writing <u>effective</u>. You'll also have to say <u>how effective</u> you think a text is at getting its <u>message</u> across to the <u>reader</u>.

> 'Text' just means a piece of writing.

> The 'reader' is just anyone who's reading the text.

Non-Fiction Texts are pieces of writing about Real Life

Non-fiction texts are about <u>real-life</u> events, people and places, e.g.

fact-sheets	information leaflets	biographies	autobiographies
travel writing	diaries	journals	

Some texts are <u>written</u> specifically for the <u>media</u>. Media texts include <u>newspaper</u> articles, <u>magazine</u> articles, <u>advertisements</u> and <u>websites</u>. Media texts are usually <u>non-fiction</u> — e.g. newspaper articles about real-life issues.

> The 'media' are types of communication that can reach large audiences, e.g. newspapers, magazines, films, websites and radio.

Although non-fiction texts are based on real life, they often contain the <u>personal opinions</u> of the writer. They might only give you <u>one version of events</u>. Don't expect a piece of writing to tell the truth and be fair to everyone just because it's non-fiction...

This book doubles up as a rather fetching hat...

This book is full of straightforward ways of getting <u>extra marks</u> in the Unit 1 exam on reading non-fiction texts. The best way to use the book is to read through the explanations and examples and practise all the tips. Then try to include as many as you can in your work.

*If you're in Wales, your exam will be structured slightly differently, but this book will still be useful. Ask your teacher for more information.

The Audience

When you're reading a non-fiction text, you've got to think about the <u>audience</u> —
the people the writer wants to read their work.

The Audience is the People who read the text

The writer will always have a <u>certain group of people</u> in mind as their audience when they write.

e.g.

TEXT	AUDIENCE
Article in 'The Financial Times'	Business people
Travel guidebook	Holiday-makers
Problem page in 'Sugar'	Teenage girls

The audience that a writer has in mind for their work is called the 'target audience'.

Content and Presentation can show who the Audience is

1) Sometimes you can work out who the audience is by the text's <u>content</u> (subject matter), e.g. an article in 'Top Gear' magazine about cars is obviously aimed at someone who's into cars.

2) The <u>presentation</u> can also tell you who the target audience is. E.g. a book with a <u>large, simple font</u> and lots of <u>pictures</u> is probably for children.

The font is the style of lettering used. There are formal fonts and informal fonts.

Language can give you plenty of clues too

1) The <u>vocabulary</u> (choice of words) can tell you about the target audience, e.g. about the <u>age group</u>:

> Today, we witnessed a discussion on foxhunting. This issue elicited mixed emotions.

Difficult vocabulary, e.g. saying 'elicited' instead of just 'brought out', shows this text is aimed at adults.

> Dungeon Killer 3 is the hottest new game of the year! There are 52 amazing levels.

Modern slang, e.g. 'hottest new game' shows this is aimed at younger people.

2) The language can also give you clues about the target audience's <u>level of understanding</u>:

> The object of a game of football is to get the ball in the opposing team's goal. It might sound easy, but it's a very skilful game.

Simple explanations show this is for beginners.

> The next hole was a par-3 and I hit my tee shot directly onto the green. Sadly my putting let me down badly and I ended up getting a bogey.

Technical words show this is for people who know a bit about the sport.

Hello? Is there anybody there?

You need to work out who the target audience is. For example, is the writer aiming their work at children? Or are they aiming it at adults? It'll have a big impact on the way the text is written.

The Purpose of the Text

Another big thing you need to work out about the texts you get in the exam is: "What is the writer's <u>purpose</u>?" In other words, "<u>Why</u> has the writer written this?" Why indeed.

There are some Common Purposes of writing

The <u>purpose</u> of the text means the <u>reason</u> that it has been written — what the writer is <u>trying to do</u>. Non-fiction texts are often written for <u>one or more</u> of these reasons:

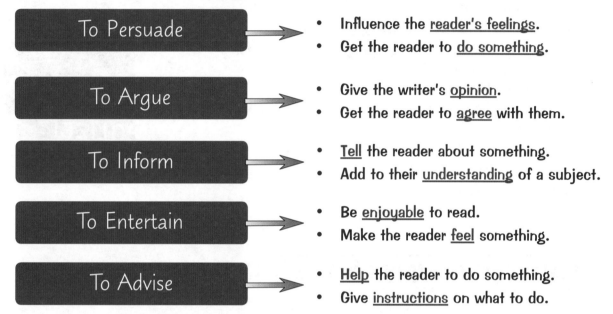

| To Persuade | → | • Influence the <u>reader's feelings</u>.
• Get the reader to <u>do something</u>. |

To Persuade →
• Influence the <u>reader's feelings</u>.
• Get the reader to <u>do something</u>.

To Argue →
• Give the writer's <u>opinion</u>.
• Get the reader to <u>agree</u> with them.

To Inform →
• <u>Tell</u> the reader about something.
• Add to their <u>understanding</u> of a subject.

To Entertain →
• Be <u>enjoyable</u> to read.
• Make the reader <u>feel</u> something.

To Advise →
• <u>Help</u> the reader to do something.
• Give <u>instructions</u> on what to do.

Pages 4-8 tell you how to spot which of these purposes the writer has in mind, and how you can <u>discuss</u> them in the exam.

You also need to know about Tone and Style

1) The different <u>tones</u> that writers can use are like the different <u>tones of voice</u> when people speak, e.g. calm, angry, friendly.
2) <u>Style</u> is to do with the type of language and techniques a writer uses, for example formal or informal.
3) Writers choose a style and tone that suits the <u>audience</u> they're writing for and the <u>purpose</u> of the writing.

There's more about tone and style on p.9-10.

When you're reading a non-fiction text, remember to think about:
• <u>who</u> the author is writing for (audience)
• what they're <u>trying to do</u> (purpose)
• <u>how</u> they write (style and tone)
• to what extent you think they <u>succeed</u>.

WARNING: Being too informal can lead to dire consequences.

My life has no purpose — but I do have a dog that barks...

Some texts have more than one purpose, e.g. travel books are often meant to entertain, as they're full of interesting stories, but they're usually informative too, telling you where to visit and where to avoid.

Texts that Persuade

Some texts have the purpose of <u>persuading</u> you to do something, like donate money to save a rare species of hamster, or something like that anyway.

Persuasive Writing tries to get you to Do Something

1) <u>Persuasive</u> writing tries to get the reader to do something, e.g. to support a charity, buy a product or try a new activity.

2) Persuasive writing often uses these <u>techniques</u>:
   - using <u>light-hearted, friendly language</u> that creates a bond with the reader
   - appealing to the reader's <u>emotions</u>
   - <u>flattering</u> the reader — trying to make the reader feel good
   - using <u>rhetorical questions</u> and <u>repetition</u> (see p.14).

3) <u>Media texts</u> are often <u>persuasive</u>, e.g. an <u>advertisement</u> persuading you to buy a new game.

It's not easy trying to persuade a policebear that historical reenactment's cool.

Persuasive writing looks like this

Tells the reader what to do. →

> The Tarnished is the best British film since Get Carter. It buzzes with fresh ideas, sharp dialogue and inspired acting. The Tarnished will be showing at art-house cinemas next week. Catch it while you can — you'll feel a fool if you miss it. Surely, this is the 'Great British Film' we have all been waiting for?

← **Uses "we" to create a bond with the reader.**

Write about texts that persuade Like This

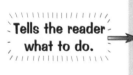

Back up your points with quotes. →

> The writer uses a rhetorical question to make the writing more persuasive: "Surely, this is the 'Great British Film' we have all been waiting for?" This question encourages the reader to have high expectations of the film, making them more likely to go and see it.

← Show that you understand the effect of the writer's techniques.

Persuasive texts are great, don't you agree? Yes you do...

There's often a persuasive text in the WJEC exam. So it's really important to understand the writing techniques used in persuasive texts and the effect these have on the reader. There's more information about these techniques in the next few sections. Keep on reading, folks...

Texts that Argue

Another common purpose of texts is to <u>argue</u> a point, to get the reader to agree with it.

Writing to Argue is all about Opinions

1) When people write to <u>argue</u>, they want to make the reader <u>agree with their opinion</u>.

2) They try to write <u>clearly</u> and <u>strongly</u> to get their points across, e.g. newspaper columnists.

3) Writing to argue <u>isn't the same</u> as having an argument with somebody. Writers will usually be <u>polite</u> when they're arguing a point — they want to get the reader <u>on their side</u>.

4) Writers use plenty of techniques to make their arguments <u>more effective</u>, e.g.

- <u>backing up</u> their argument with facts and statistics
- using <u>quotes from experts</u> who agree with their argument
- explaining why <u>other points of view</u> are wrong
- using <u>repetition</u> and <u>rhetorical questions</u> (see p.14).

Writing to Argue looks like this

People who claim that young people are lazy are guilty of both prejudice and ignorance. The vast majority of young people are very hard-working. In a recent survey of 14-16 year olds, 76% said they had a Saturday job and another 6% did weekday paper rounds. Does that sound like laziness to you?

Opinions clear from the start.

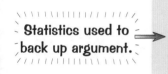 **Statistics used to back up argument.**

Rhetorical question (see p.14) challenges the reader to think about the issue.

Write about texts that argue Like This

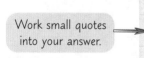 Work small quotes into your answer.

The writer argues his point very forcefully. He uses statistics to show that many young people have jobs and accuses those who disagree with him of "prejudice and ignorance". This suggests that anyone who thinks young people are lazy has not really thought the issue through.

Show how the writer's argument works.

I h8 U — I h8 U 2...

If a writer is trying to argue a point, it's all about getting the reader to see things from their point of view. It won't be balanced, like a discussion — it'll be one-sided, with evidence that's carefully chosen because it supports their point of view.

Texts that Inform

If the purpose of a text is to <u>inform</u>, the writer's aim is to tell you something as clearly as possible. Informative texts have lots of <u>facts</u> and usually a <u>straightforward style</u>.

Informative Writing Tells You <u>something</u>

Informative texts give the reader <u>facts and information</u>. This could be:

- <u>what has happened</u> — e.g. a news article or a history book
- <u>what will or might happen</u> — e.g. a weather forecast
- <u>something you might need to know</u> — e.g. a **TV guide** or **travel guide**

Informative Writing <u>looks like this</u>

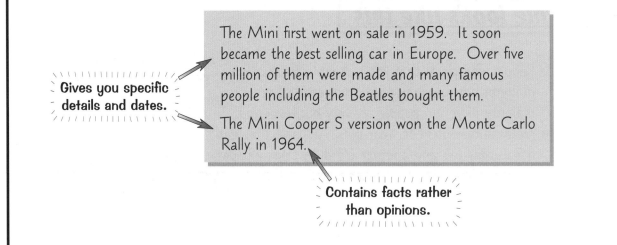

Gives you specific details and dates.

> The Mini first went on sale in 1959. It soon became the best selling car in Europe. Over five million of them were made and many famous people including the Beatles bought them.
>
> The Mini Cooper S version won the Monte Carlo Rally in 1964.

Contains facts rather than opinions.

Write about informative texts Like This

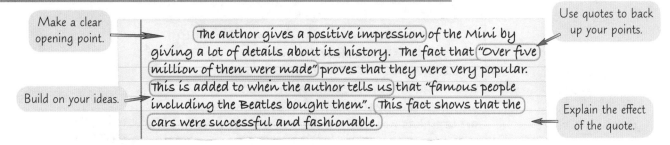

Make a clear opening point.

Build on your ideas.

> The author gives a positive impression of the Mini by giving a lot of details about its history. The fact that "Over five million of them were made" proves that they were very popular. This is added to when the author tells us that "famous people including the Beatles bought them". This fact shows that the cars were successful and fashionable.

Use quotes to back up your points.

Explain the effect of the quote.

If there are lots of facts and figures, it's informative...

You need to show you can recognise informative writing and explain how it's used. Think about what the writer is informing us about, why they're doing it and how effective they are.

Entertaining Texts

Entertaining writing is stuff that you would read for <u>pleasure</u>. It has lots of the kind of things that make you <u>scared</u>, <u>excited</u> or <u>amused</u>. That's more of the fun stuff, then...

Entertaining Writing aims to be Enjoyable to read

1) Entertaining writing is meant to be <u>interesting</u>. People read it for <u>fun</u>.
   Travel books are a good example of entertaining non-fiction writing.

2) The author might entertain the reader with stories of <u>funny things</u> that happened to them.
   Or they might use <u>entertaining descriptions</u> of things or people.

3) Entertaining writing has more <u>creative</u> and <u>unexpected</u> bits than informative writing.

Entertaining Writing looks like this

This piece of writing is on the same subject as the one on page 6 — but this one is <u>entertaining</u>. Have a look at how it's different from the informative one.

> My first car was a 1970 Mini. I loved it from the moment I sat in it. It went like a rocket. By that I mean it always had smoke coming out of its rear end! Perhaps I shouldn't have tried to drive it like Michael Caine.
>
> It was a subtle shade of bright orange and should have come complete with free executive sunglasses. Still, I was a student then and they wouldn't have fitted my image.

Interesting comparisons.

Contains funny images.

Tells a story about real life.

Write about entertaining texts Like This

Make an opening point.

The author gains the reader's attention by writing in the first person ("I"). That makes her experiences seem more real. She uses humour to maintain interest. For example "it always had smoke coming out of its rear end!" creates a comical picture and makes the writing more entertaining.

Use evidence from the text.

Remember to explain the effect of the quote.

Nobby found the new Bill Bryson book most entertaining.

Writing exam answers — now that's entertainment...

Some texts will be both informative and entertaining, e.g. a travel book may contain useful facts about a place but also give you some funny stories about what happened when the author was there. Try to work out which bits of the text inform and which entertain when you write about them.

Texts that Advise

When people write to advise, they're trying to help the reader to <u>do something</u>, or to make the right <u>decision</u>. The style is more straightforward and less emotional than writing that argues or persuades.

Writing to Advise sounds Clear and Calm

1) When people are writing to advise, they want their readers to <u>follow their suggestions</u>.

2) The tone will be <u>calm</u> and <u>less emotional</u> than writing that argues or persuades.

3) The advice will usually be <u>clearly written and laid out</u>. The writer may use bullet points or numbered lists to make it easier to follow.

4) There are lots of different types of texts which advise — ranging from <u>magazine problem pages</u> to <u>health advice leaflets</u>.

"Congratulations on purchasing your new TS-522/A shell..."

Writing to Advise looks like this

Talks to the reader by using the second person ("you").

> Before you buy a pension, you need to be sure that it is the right one for you. You should look at the pension company's reputation, past results and penalties for changing schemes.

Uses details to give useful advice.

Write about texts that advise Like This

Use P.E.E. in your answers — Point, Example, Explanation. See page 28.

This is your point...

> The writer uses a friendly, no-nonsense tone to get her advice across clearly. When she says, "you need to be sure", it sounds as if she is talking to a friend. This makes the reader more likely to take the advice.
>
> The details of the advice, such as "look at the pension company's reputation", make the writer seem to know a lot about the subject. As a result of this, the reader is more likely to think that the advice is worthwhile.

... here's your example...

... and this bit explains the effect of language on the reader.

Texts that advise are clearly presented and easy to follow

Texts that advise generally assume you're already on the writer's side — people usually choose to read them because they want to know about something and they trust the writer's opinion. Because of this, they usually sound more friendly and less "in-your-face" than texts that argue or persuade.

Formal Writing

Formal writing sounds polite or "correct" — the sort of thing you'd use in schoolwork.
It tends to use an impersonal tone — the writer doesn't try to be matey.

There are a few ways of Spotting Formal Writing

1) It's quite easy to recognise a formal style of writing. Just think about the way a letter from your teacher or a newspaper article would be written.

2) Here are a few common features of formal writing:

- a dry or "stuffy" tone (not exciting or emotional)
- standard English — no slang or abbreviations
- long, complex sentences with correct punctuation
- sounds impersonal — the writer doesn't try to relate to you
- written in the third person — "he", "she", "they" etc.
- you don't get a sense of the writer's personality
- no jokes or light-hearted comments

When the writer mentioned 'pâté' for the third time, Jeremy felt it related to him just a little too much.

3) Pieces of writing that are usually written in a formal style include:

- textbooks
- charity appeals
- business letters
- instruction manuals
- news reports
- job adverts

Formal Writing looks like this

Long sentence. →

Avoids shortened words — "it is" instead of "it's". →

> When wiring an electrical plug it is always necessary to follow the safety instructions in order to avoid personal injury or death. It is easy to suffer serious harm. Therefore, ignoring the instructions is simply not worth the risk. Some people believe that it is better to leave this kind of work to qualified electricians.

← **Sounds strict.**

← **Opinion is given in an impersonal tone.**

Write about formal writing Like This

Say what style the writer uses.

Give an example.

> The writer creates a formal style by using long sentences and avoiding talking directly to the reader. For example, he says "it is always necessary to" instead of "you have to". The formal style helps to add to the impact of the information. I think it is effective because it gives an impression of how dangerous it would be if you did not follow the advice.

Show how the formal style works.

Say if you think it works and why.

One is undoubtedly required to discuss formal writing...

Basically, if a text sounds like it's been written by a teacher or a bank manager, it's formal. As usual, you need to say why the writer has chosen to use this style and tone — think about who they're writing for and what message they're trying to give, and say how the formal style helps them do this.

Informal Writing

Informal writing sounds as if someone is <u>chatting</u> to you. It sounds more friendly and casual than formal writing. Writers use a <u>personal tone</u> to try to build up a relationship with the reader.

Informal Writing *sounds chatty*

1) If writing is clearly <u>not formal</u>, it's — wait for it — <u>informal</u>. Tricky eh?

2) Here are a few common <u>features</u> of informal writing:

> • a chatty, personal tone — as if the writer is talking to you
> • written in the first person — "I", "me", "my" etc.
> • a sense of the author's personality, opinions and emotions
> • non-standard English — e.g. abbreviations and slang
> • short, simple sentences
> • jokes and a light-hearted tone

Light-hearted Tone was a perfect match for Carefree Meg.

3) Pieces of writing that are often written in an <u>informal style</u> include:

- teenage magazine articles
- adverts aimed at young people
- letters between friends
- gossip columns
- travel writing
- autobiographies

Informal Writing *looks like this*

Personal opinion.

Written in first person.

> School uniform should be banned. As if it isn't bad enough wearing a manky, itchy jumper most of the time, the PE kit we have to wear was designed for the 1950s. Mine was bought in Year 7 and it's ridiculously tight now. Then in Science, the lab coat and safety goggles make me look like a short-sighted lollipop lady.

Use of humour emphasises personal voice.

Write *about informal writing Like This*

Say what effect the personal style has.

> The informal style allows the writer to express her views very directly and forcefully. By writing in the first person, she seems to be speaking directly to the reader. She says her science clothes "make me look like a short-sighted lollipop lady". This humorous image shows how silly the uniform is and highlights the writer's feelings of embarrassment.

Use the correct technical terms.

Explain why the quote is effective.

Informal writing helps the reader relate to the writer...

The formality or informality of a piece of writing is all about how it's written, rather than what it actually says. Remember to explain who the writing is aimed at (audience), what the writer is trying to do (purpose), how the writer is trying to do it, and how well you think the writer has done it.

Features of an Argument

If you're going to talk about a writer's argument in your answer, the first thing you need to do is <u>follow</u> the argument — in other words, <u>understand what points they're making</u>.

Look out for the Main Features of an Argument

A writer can use lots of different <u>techniques</u> when they argue a point. They could include:

*   <u>facts</u> which back up their argument.
*   <u>opinions</u> — either the author's or someone else's.
*   <u>implications</u> — where the writer suggests something is the case without saying it outright, e.g. "Ever since Kevin moved in, things have started mysteriously disappearing."
*   <u>rhetoric</u> and <u>bias</u> — see page 14.

You have to be able to spot <u>when</u> one of these features turns up in the text, and say what <u>effect</u> it has.

Identify the Key Points of the argument

To follow an argument, you need to work out what the <u>key points</u> are — the main reasons the writer gives to back up their argument.

You can often spot where each new key point begins by the writer's use of paragraphs. A <u>new paragraph</u> often means a <u>new key point</u>:

> In this increasingly stressful age it is important that young people find the time to relax and enjoy the best years of their life. With exam after exam, modern teenagers hardly have time to take a break and have fun with their friends.
>
> On top of the demands from school, the attitudes of demanding parents often do not help. The constant query of "Have you done your biology revision yet?" can only add to the stress and frustration of having to give up the opportunity of fun for more schoolwork.

The key point of the first paragraph is that exams can prevent teenagers from enjoying themselves.

The key point of the second paragraph is how parents can put pressure on teenagers.

Another way of spotting where a new point starts is when you see <u>linking words and phrases</u>:

| however | secondly | furthermore | on the other hand | in addition |

Taxi! Follow that argument...

If you try to talk about the whole text in one go, you'll more than likely end up in a sticky mess on the floor. But if you break an argument down into its main points, you'll find it a lot easier to discuss how the writer makes their points and how effective they are — see next page...

Evaluating an Argument

Evaluating an argument means saying how <u>effective</u> it is. You need to say whether or not you think it will persuade the reader to agree with the writer, and why.

Say What's Good about the argument

1) It's <u>not enough</u> just to say an argument is good. You need to say <u>how</u> the writer makes their points and explain <u>why</u> they're effective.

2) Think about what kind of <u>impression</u> (e.g. forceful, emotional, knowledgeable) the writer creates with the language they use, and <u>how</u> this impression helps to <u>persuade</u> the reader.

When Carl wanted to make an impression, he let his jumper do the talking.

Evaluate an argument Like This

Talk about one technique at a time.

One reason that the argument is effective is the writer's use of adjectives. For example, negative words such as "stressful" are used to describe the difficulties teenagers face. These adjectives show that students find the amount of schoolwork difficult to cope with.

Give an example.

Say why the technique is effective.

The argument might have some Drawbacks

You might think some parts of an argument don't work very well, and if that's what you reckon, <u>say so</u>. But if you do say this, make sure you've got some darn good <u>reasons</u> for saying so — if you just say, "the writer's argument is really stupid, he's missed the point", you won't get good marks.

Here are some criticisms you might be able to make:

1) <u>Confusing writing</u> — a writer might say things which <u>contradict</u> each other.

2) <u>Inaccurate information</u> — the writer's information might just be plain <u>wrong</u>. Watch out though — you have to be sure you really know your stuff before you go saying something's wrong.

3) <u>Dullness</u> — sometimes an argument just won't grab you. This might be because it's <u>full of statistics</u> and not much else, or because the text is <u>repetitive</u> or <u>unclear</u>. As always, if you can <u>give examples</u> of this, you'll pick up marks.

It was terrible! It wasn't that bad! It was great! MORE!

In your exam, you might be given a text that's presenting an argument. You need to be able to analyse the text by evaluating the argument and saying how successful it is. It's usually easiest to say mostly good things, but try to include one or two criticisms too, to make your answer balanced.

Facts and Opinions

Some arguments use <u>facts</u> and <u>opinions</u>. You need to be able to say what effect they have.

Facts <u>are definitely</u> True...

FACT: Manchester United won the UEFA Champions League in May 2008.

FACT: Barack Obama was the President of the United States after George W. Bush.

Write about facts Like This

This is an answer to a question about sporting champions:

Make your point.

You could use "for example" to start your examples.

> The author uses facts in the text to strengthen his argument that Carl Lewis is the greatest sprinter and long jumper in history. For example, he mentions Lewis's nine Olympic gold medals, two world records for the 100 metres, and 65 consecutive long jump competition victories. Each fact proves the author's point about how successful Lewis was.

Explain why the author has used facts.

Opinions aren't True or Untrue — they're just Beliefs

Opinions are just what someone <u>thinks</u>.
You <u>can't prove</u> that an opinion is true or untrue.

The words "I think" show that this is just a point of view.

OPINION: I think that animal testing for cosmetics should be banned.

OPINION: CD singles won't exist in 10 years' time.

You can't prove this one way or the other yet, even though it sounds like a fact.

Write about opinions Like This

Mention the effect the opinions have.

> The author uses strongly-worded opinions to mock people she does not like. For example: "Jamie Pullan comes second only to my three-year-old nephew in the contest for the world's most irritating display of chirpiness." The humour of these opinions creates an image in the reader's mind, making the author's argument more persuasive.

Explain what it is about the opinion that makes it effective.

In my opinion, Hugh Jackman is extremely good-looking...

If a text gives different opinions, you might need to compare them. There are a few phrases that often come in handy for this. Here's a few: similar to, contrasting with, on the other hand, different from, however, in agreement with, unlike, in the same way, conversely. All very useful.

Rhetoric and Bias

Writers use <u>rhetoric</u> and <u>bias</u> to make their arguments more <u>convincing</u>.

Rhetoric _is about_ Influencing _the readers'_ Opinions

1) <u>Rhetorical questions</u> don't need an <u>answer</u> — they're phrased to make the answer seem so <u>obvious</u> it's not even worth saying.

2) This makes the reader feel like they're <u>making their own mind up</u>, when actually the writer is deliberately trying to get them to think a <u>certain way</u>.

> Can it really be fair to set students these ridiculous and unnecessary assignments?

The words "ridiculous" and "unnecessary" are put there to get the reader to think, "No, of course it's not fair."

3) Another rhetorical technique writers use is <u>repetition</u>. Writers <u>repeat</u> words or phrases to <u>emphasise</u> their most important points. They're often repeated in <u>threes</u> (called the <u>rule-of-three</u>).

> It's <u>outrageous</u> to suggest that pupils don't work hard. It's <u>outrageous</u> to make us give up all our free time for study. Most of all, it's <u>outrageous</u> to expect us to take on even more homework.

Write _about rhetoric_ Like This

> The writer uses rhetoric to persuade the reader that students should not be given more homework to do. For example, his repetition of the word "outrageous" emphasises how awful more homework would be.

Say what effect the repeated word has — don't assume it's obvious.

Biased Writing _is affected by the writer's opinions_

1) A biased text <u>doesn't</u> give a <u>balanced</u> view — the <u>writer's own point of view</u> affects the writing.

2) The writer might <u>exaggerate</u> things that support their argument, or <u>not mention</u> things that oppose it.

3) You need to be able to <u>recognise</u> bias, so that you don't confuse opinions with facts.

> Coldplay are the best band to ever come out of this country. They have produced hit after hit, and perform to huge sell-out crowds.

- The first sentence is just <u>opinion</u> — lots of people might completely <u>disagree</u> with this.
- The text <u>ignores</u> the fact that many other bands have lots of hits and play to big audiences.

Write _about bias_ Like This

Make a clear opening point.

Say what the overall effect of the bias is.

> The writer is clearly biased in favour of Coldplay. He mentions "hit after hit" and "huge sell-out crowds", but does not give any details. This clear bias makes the writer's argument less convincing as he appears to have made his opinion without finding any proper evidence for it.

Support it with quotes.

Exams are great, exams are great, exams are great...

There are lots of other <u>rhetorical techniques</u>, for example using emotive language (see page 24) or implications (suggesting something without saying it outright) to add to the text's impact.

Headlines and Subheadings

Presentational devices are used to make the page layout more interesting. You need to be able to say what specific __effects__ they have. The beauty of them is that their effects are actually pretty obvious.

Headlines and Subheadings help organise the text

1) Headlines tell you <u>what</u> the article is <u>about</u>.

2) In newspapers and magazines, headlines are always <u>bigger</u> than the other words, and are at the <u>top</u> of the page.

3) Headlines capture your <u>interest</u>, so you'll read the article. They sometimes use <u>humour</u>, <u>exaggeration</u> or <u>shocking facts</u> to grab your attention.

1) <u>Subheadings</u> are used to <u>split</u> the story up into little pieces to make it look <u>easier to read</u>.

2) Each subheading briefly tells you <u>what</u> the next section of text is about.

3) They're usually a bit <u>bigger</u> than the rest of the text and might be <u>bold</u> or <u>underlined</u> to make them stand out.

Headlines and Subheadings look like this

CHANTELLE'S SECRET WEDDING SHOCKER

Private ceremony for TV's golden girl

By our showbiz reporter, Jane Snooping

Pop TV starlet Chantelle Williams has caused controversy by privately marrying her secret boyfriend Barry at a quiet ceremony in the Lake District.

CHANTELLE LOOKED BEAUTIFUL
According to insiders, the blonde bombshell was 'really excited' to be tying the knot with her childhood sweetheart. She looked beautiful in a traditional white laced gown and veil, carrying a bouquet of lilies.

Chantelle and Barry

FORMER BOYFRIEND IS 'APPALLED'
Former boyfriend and rock star, Parker, was apparently 'shocked and appalled' by the secret marriage. He refused to comment to The Daily Gossip, but insiders hinted that he was distraught.

COUPLE TO HONEYMOON IN CARIBBEAN
After their secret wedding, the couple jetted off on honeymoon to the beautiful island paradise of Antigua. They will stay at a luxury beach resort for two weeks before returning to London to set up their new home.

This is the headline.

These are the subheadings.

Write about headlines and subheadings Like This

The headline, "Chantelle's Secret Wedding Shocker", gets the reader's attention. For example, the word "secret" will interest readers because it hints that new information will be revealed.

The subheadings guide the reader through the article, making it clear what each section is talking about. For example, the subheading "Couple to Honeymoon in Caribbean" tells the reader that the next paragraph is about the couple's honeymoon plans.

Don't forget to quote, even when it seems obvious.

Expand your point to show exactly what you mean.

Subheadings — send in the substitute headteacher...

Headlines are there to attract your attention, so on some newspapers they're really big. If the headline's about something really exciting, it could be three inches tall — this makes it really stand out against its competitors on the newspaper stand when people are deciding which paper to buy.

Graphics and Captions

"Graphics" is just a posh word for <u>pictures</u>. Graphics are often used to grab the reader's attention, back up the information in the text and make the meaning of the text clearer.

Graphics and Captions give us lots of Information

1) Texts often have graphics, e.g. photos, illustrations, diagrams, graphs and charts, to <u>show what they're about</u>.

2) They usually have <u>captions</u> with them — a short bit of text to explain what the graphic shows.

3) <u>Colourful graphics</u> can make the text look <u>more attractive</u> to the reader.

Graphics and Captions look like this

Hurricane causes devastation

A lifetime of fun and affection — take me home

Friday, 9.00am

The photo shows more about the awful effects of the hurricane than the text alone could.

This picture is persuasive — the cute puppy is meant to make the reader feel a bit soppy.

The caption clarifies what's being shown — it tells you when the weather forecast is for.

Write about graphics and captions Like This

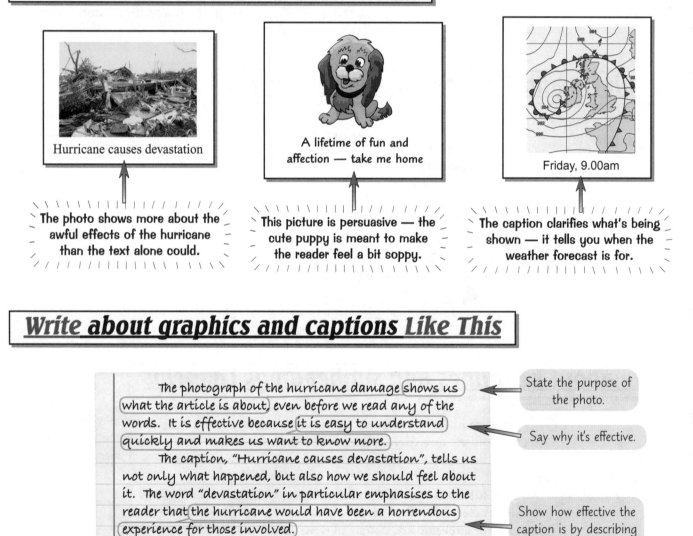

The photograph of the hurricane damage shows us what the article is about, even before we read any of the words. It is effective because it is easy to understand quickly and makes us want to know more.
    The caption, "Hurricane causes devastation", tells us not only what happened, but also how we should feel about it. The word "devastation" in particular emphasises to the reader that the hurricane would have been a horrendous experience for those involved.

State the purpose of the photo.

Say why it's effective.

Show how effective the caption is by describing its effect on the reader.

Think about why a particular picture's been used...

Remember, the graphic always goes with the words in the article. It shows us what the article is about. Don't just say what the graphic is — say <u>why</u> it's effective and how it connects to the text.

Text Columns and Text Boxes

Now you know how writers can grab your attention, you need to be able to talk about how they keep you interested. Text columns and boxes are two of their little ploys.

Boxes and Columns are ways of Presenting Text

1) Writers sometimes break their text up into columns — it makes it appear shorter and easier to read.

2) You see text columns all over the place — in magazines, newspapers, adverts etc.

1) Sometimes part of a text is put in a box to make it grab your attention.

2) The box can be made to stand out even more by making it a strong colour, or putting it at an angle.

Text Columns and Text Boxes look like this

THE DAILY GOSSIP

PIG FARMER SUES PIG OVER FALSE ALLEGATIONS

WOMEN SWIM INTO RECORD BOOKS

NEW FEATURE

These columns make the text look short and easy to read.

WOW! fashion fame beauty

Even skinnier!!!

Kate

Real-life horror stories inside!!!

35p!

Brightly coloured and angled boxes make the text stand out.

Write about text columns and text boxes Like This

Columns have been used in the newspaper article to make the text easy to follow. The columns break down the long article about the pig farmer, making it appear shorter than if it was presented in a single block of text.

In the magazine, text boxes have been used to draw attention to key pieces of information. For example, the low price of the magazine has been highlighted in an eye-catching yellow box. This would attract a reader's attention and might persuade them to buy the magazine.

Show you know how the text columns work.

Remember to write about the effect these features have on the reader.

Bruno and Tyson compete via mobile phone...

If you don't really get it, just think about a magazine without any columns or boxes. Imagine that all the writing just went from left to right in a giant block across the page. It'd be tricky to read — people would be scared away by the amount of text. Columns and boxes are clever little tricks really.

Bullet Points and Numbered Lists

Now that you understand how text boxes and text columns work, it's time to look at other devices that writers use to make sure their work is clearly presented and easy to understand.

Bullet Points and Numbered Lists break texts down

1) Bullet points are dots, dashes or other symbols that go at the start of each new point in a list.

2) Sometimes lists can be numbered instead. This is useful when writers want to put their points into a particular order.

3) Bullet points and numbered lists are often used when writers want to give you lots of information. They separate information into step-by-step points, to make it easier to read.

Bullet Points and Numbered Lists look like this

The scuba diving course covers:
- Equipment care
- Breathing from a regulator
- Caring for the environment
- Being safe

Dots are often used as bullet points.

Before your exam make sure that you:
1. Know where and when the exam is.
2. Get a good night's sleep.
3. Get up in time to have breakfast.
4. Have everything you need for the exam.

This is a numbered list.

I'm sure there was something I had to do today...

Tracy had forgotten point 5 — do the exam.

Write about bullet points and numbered lists Like This

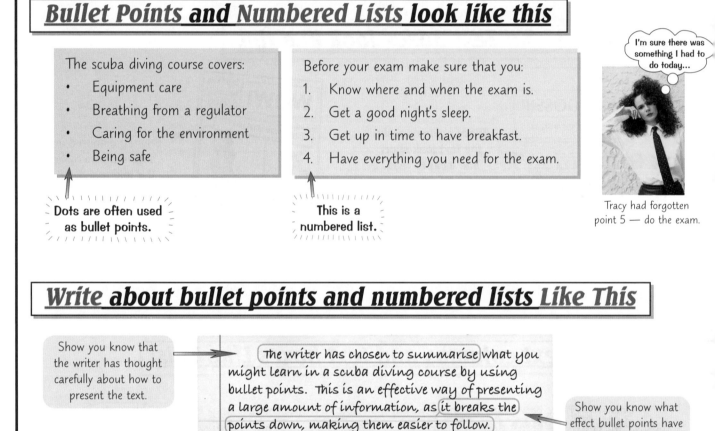

Show you know that the writer has thought carefully about how to present the text.

The writer has chosen to summarise what you might learn in a scuba diving course by using bullet points. This is an effective way of presenting a large amount of information, as it breaks the points down, making them easier to follow.

In the second example, the writer presents his advice as a numbered list. The use of numbers emphasises the order in which the advice should be followed. It also reassures the reader by giving the impression that there is only a limited amount of information to remember.

Show you know what effect bullet points have on the reader.

Show you understand that the numbers are there for a reason.

My bullet points didn't work — they must've been blanks...

OK, it doesn't take a genius to spot a bullet point, but it's still worth writing about them. Show the examiner that you understand the effect different ways of presenting text can have on the reader. You can get yourself a couple of extra marks — which is always nice.

Font Styles and Formatting

You need to remember that everything on a page tells you something about the text. This includes what the writing looks like.

Fonts are different Styles of printed text

1) The <u>font</u> of a text gives you a clue about <u>what kind</u> of text it is.
2) Serious, formal fonts are for <u>serious</u>, formal texts.
3) Cartoony fonts are for <u>light-hearted</u> texts, or texts for <u>children</u>.

Fonts can be <u>formatted</u>, e.g. by making them **bold** or *italic*, <u>underlining</u> them or putting them in CAPITALS.

Writers format fonts to make particular words <u>stand out</u>.

The mischievous smile meant she'd written her speech in Litterbox ICG again.

Here are some examples of Different Fonts

This font is formal and sets a serious tone.

This font is informal and easy to read.

This font looks quirky and old-fashioned.

Font Formatting looks like this

WOMEN SWIM INTO RECORD BOOKS

At 10pm last night, the last of the **5,000** female swimmers arrived at Calais, having set off from Dover at 5am. This marks the largest group swim ever in the history of swimming.

The women together have raised over **a million pounds** for a variety of charities. They plan to repeat the event next year, and hopefully will double their number.

The event's organiser, Gill Potts, said, *"I'm really pleased with everyone's effort. They had to swim through two miles of jellyfish, but not one of them complained."*

Waiting at Calais was Robbie Williams, who had promised a **kiss** for each swimmer to arrive. When told that 5,000 women were approaching the shore, the singer was apparently *"a little shocked"*.

Could <u>you</u> swim the channel? Visit <u>www.swimmingisgreat.uk.png</u> for details on next year's event.

Capital letters are often used for headings.

Italics can be used to highlight quotes.

Underlining can be used to highlight important words.

Bold is useful for highlighting important words.

Write about fonts Like This

The newspaper article uses a formal font. This creates a serious tone appropriate for a news article. The font is clear and easy to read, making the long article less intimidating to the reader.

One of the writer's intentions is to make readers realise how much money was raised. This is made really clear as "a million pounds" is printed in bold, making it stand out.

You don't need to know the names of the fonts — just describe them.

Remember to explain the effect of the formatting.

I'd like to do some formatting, if I may be so bold...

Remember, the font tells you about the tone of the text at first glance. So a serious, boring font tells you that the text is probably very formal and is not a laughing matter. A silly, cartoony font tells you that the text is light-hearted, jokey and informal. It's not rocket science, this font stuff.

Descriptive Language

The texts you have to write about in the exam will use lots of different language techniques to make them more effective. You need to be able to recognise the techniques and say why they're used.

Descriptive Language makes text Interesting

1) Descriptive language includes imagery such as metaphors, similes and personification (see page 21).

2) Writers often give descriptions based on their five senses.

3) Another sign of descriptive language is when the writer uses lots of adjectives — describing words like "huge" or "fiery".

4) Descriptive language creates a picture in the reader's mind. It also makes the text more interesting, dramatic and real.

- what they can see
- what they can smell
- what they can hear
- what they can feel or touch
- what they can taste

EXAMPLE   After the dreary, grey sheet of rain had swept over the land, the parched, sun-baked fields transformed into a fertile, emerald-green valley.

Write about descriptive language Like This

The writer uses descriptive language to describe the effect of the rains on the African landscape. He uses adjectives such as "parched" and "sun-baked" to describe the dry fields before the rain and contrasts them with the bright "emerald-green valley" after the rain. This allows the reader to picture how dramatic the changes that the rains bring are.

Here are your examples.

Explain why the writer has used descriptive language.

Don't do it like this

The writer uses lots of descriptive language which makes it more interesting.

Don't just say it makes it more interesting.

To get the marks, you need to say why the descriptive language makes the text more interesting for the reader.

As he read the first draft of Amy's novel, Darryl tried desperately to think of another word for "interesting".

My dad used descriptive language when I broke his mug...

It's not too hard to get the hang of writing about these techniques — just spot where one's been used, quote it, and explain how it's been used deliberately to affect the reader in some way. Easy.

Metaphors, Similes and Personification

Metaphors, similes and personification are all types of <u>imagery</u> (see p.50).

Metaphors, similes and personification are Comparisons

Metaphors, similes and personification describe one thing by <u>comparing</u> it to something else.

<u>Metaphors</u> describe something by saying that it <u>is</u> something else.

EXAMPLE I tried to run but my feet <u>were</u> blocks of concrete.

<u>Similes</u> describe something by saying that it's <u>like</u> something else. They usually use the words <u>as</u> or <u>like</u>.

EXAMPLE The humid Italian air clings to my skin <u>like</u> a warm, wet blanket.

<u>Personification</u> means describing something <u>as if it's a person</u> or an <u>animal</u>.

EXAMPLE The helicopter's menacing <u>growl</u> frightened the crowd.

Write about metaphors Like This

Here's your point, made right at the start of your paragraph.

Here's your explanation.

The journalist uses a metaphor when reporting from the war zone, "I tried to run but my feet were blocks of concrete". This direct comparison gives the reader a sense of the situation being so frightening that he could not even move to run away.

Here's your example.

Write about similes Like This

This quote is tucked neatly into the sentence.

By using the simile "like a warm, wet blanket" to describe the Italian air, the writer creates a vivid feeling of just how unpleasantly damp and sticky it is.

Write about personification Like This

Say what impression the personification creates.

The writer's use of personification makes the helicopter appear threatening. Describing it as having a "menacing growl" makes it sound like a dangerous wild animal.

Use quotes to back up your points.

The spectre of the exam lurked like an invisible tiger...

Metaphors — his breath was ice, my boss is a pussycat really, your trainers are pure cheese.
Similes — his breath was as cold as ice, my boss is as nice as a cat, your trainers smell like cheese.

Alliteration and Onomatopoeia

Alliteration and onomatopoeia are used as sound effects in writing to keep readers interested.

Alliteration means repeating the same Sound

Alliteration is when words that are close together begin with the same sound. It makes the sentence seem more interesting to the reader. Alliteration is often found in headlines:

P.M.'s Panic   Rooney Rules the Roost   Close Call for Kids   Magic Murray Marches On

In the exam you'll need to identify alliteration and write about how and why it's been used.

Write about alliteration Like This

The alliteration of "Magic Murray Marches On" attracts the reader's attention to the article on Andy Murray at Wimbledon. Alliteration emphasises the headline and gives the article a snappy opening which adds to the reader's interest.

Here's the example.

Don't forget to expand your explanation to describe the effects on the reader.

Onomatopoeia means using words that Imitate Noises

Onomatopoeia means using words that sound like the noises being described. This makes the description of the sounds more dramatic and effective. Here are some good examples:

Thud   Slurp   Crackle   Smash   Tinkle   Screech   Hiss   Squish

Write about onomatopoeia Like This

Remember the effect on the reader.

The onomatopoeia of "slurp" in the cartoon used in the milkshake advertisement makes the audience recognise the humorous noise often made by children when they drink. This makes the product seem more fun and appealing to the children the text is aimed at.

Here's the example.

Think about the purpose of the text when you're writing about onomatopoeia.

Onomatopoeia — what a stupid word...

Learn how to spell ON-O-MAT-O-POEI-A. You'll impress the examiner if you can spell it correctly. It's hard, I know, but just write it out a few times and you'll get the hang of it eventually.

Irony and Sarcasm

Irony and sarcasm are techniques that are related to the <u>tone</u> of the writing (see p.51).

Irony *is saying the* Opposite *of what you* Mean

1) <u>Irony</u> is when someone <u>says one thing</u>, but <u>means</u> the <u>opposite</u>.

2) Irony is often <u>humorous</u> or <u>light-hearted</u>, but sometimes it is used to make a <u>serious</u> point.

3) Irony can be really obvious, but sometimes it's <u>less easy</u> to spot.

| EXAMPLE | We were stranded at the airport for 48 hours with no food, which was just great. |

Of course, the writer doesn't <u>really</u> mean it was great. In fact, he means it was the <u>opposite</u> of great.

Write *about irony Like This*

Here's your point. Say <u>why</u> the writer has used irony.

The writer uses irony to express his frustration at having his flight delayed. When he says that being there for 48 hours with no food was "just great" he actually means the opposite — the experience was depressing and annoying.

Here's your explanation.

Sarcasm *is* Nastier *than irony*

1) <u>Sarcasm</u> is language that has a <u>mocking</u> or <u>scornful</u> tone.

2) It's often intended to <u>insult a person</u> or <u>make fun</u> of them, or to show that the writer is <u>angry</u> about something.

3) Sarcastic writing often uses <u>irony</u> — but the tone is more <u>aggressive</u> and <u>unpleasant</u>.

| EXAMPLE | The council's latest brainwave on tackling petty crime is to take away the few local facilities available to youngsters. This is presumably intended to encourage them to stay indoors watching Hollyoaks rather than engaging with society in any way. |

Write *about sarcasm Like This*

The writer's use of sarcasm in describing the council's "brainwave" shows how stupid he thinks it is. His sarcastic comment that it is "presumably intended" to exclude young people from society suggests that the council has not thought it through.

Explain the intended effect of the sarcasm.

Sarcasm, yeah right, what a great technique...

Keep a look out for irony and sarcasm in the reading texts. If a writer says something like, "I just love waiting in long queues to buy mouldy, out-of-date yoghurt", you shouldn't take them literally.

Technical and Emotive Language

Some of the texts in the exam might use technical language to sound knowledgeable and add detail. Others may use more emotive language to try to persuade you to take their point of view.

Technical language is often used to Support an argument

1) Technical language includes things like specialist terms, jargon and statistics (see glossary). It gives an impression of the writer having in-depth knowledge of the topic they're writing about.

2) You'll find technical language in textbooks, instructions, reports, and even newspaper articles.

3) It's often used to present facts to support an argument, making it more convincing to the reader.

> **EXAMPLE** Governments need to act now to combat climate change. Average worldwide temperatures have increased by about 1°C in the last hundred years, mainly due to increased emission of greenhouse gases such as carbon dioxide and methane.

Write about technical language Like This

You won't pick up many marks if you forget to quote.

By including technical terms relating to climate change, such as "Average worldwide temperatures" and "greenhouse gases", the writer gives the impression that he understands the more complex details of the issue. He seems to know the exact nature of the problems, and this supports his argument that governments need to take more action to deal with climate change.

Explain how technical language makes the writer's argument more convincing.

Emotive language is used to Persuade

1) Writers use emotive language to get the reader to feel really strongly about something. This could be feelings of disgust, sadness, happiness, anger or any other emotion.

2) Language is often made emotive by strong adjectives, e.g. "shocking", "shameful" or "heroic".

3) Emotive language can emphasise a point — it usually makes the writer's opinion very clear.

> **EXAMPLE** The bears are forced to perform these painful dances and are frequently subjected to physical abuse.

Write about emotive language Like This

The leaflet against animal cruelty uses very emotive language. The words "forced" and "painful" are used to persuade the reader to feel, as the writer does, that this treatment is inhumane and unjustifiable.

Say how the emotive language is used.

Here comes the science...

Two more types of language to learn here, but nothing too hard to get your head around. Technical language can be used to give detail, but more often than not it's there to make the author sound like they know what they're on about. And emotive language makes you emotional. Tricky eh?

Structure

"Structure" means the way different parts of a text are put together.

Introductions create Interest in the text

1) An introduction should <u>briefly</u> give the reader the <u>main points</u> of the article.
2) It should also try to capture the reader's <u>interest</u> so that they read the <u>rest</u> of the article.

e.g. Fears were voiced last night for the safety of the lone whale who was spotted in the Thames by the Embankment in Central London. Onlookers have nicknamed him "Fred" and have taken to the banks of the river to watch.

Emotive language makes the reader want to find out more.

Gives the main points.

Write about introductions Like This

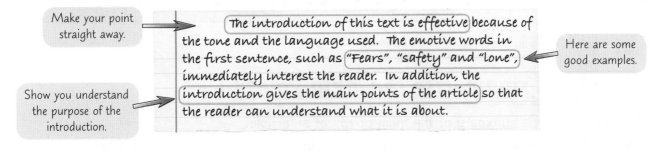

Make your point straight away.

The introduction of this text is effective because of the tone and the language used. The emotive words in the first sentence, such as "Fears", "safety" and "lone", immediately interest the reader. In addition, the introduction gives the main points of the article so that the reader can understand what it is about.

Here are some good examples.

Show you understand the purpose of the introduction.

The middle tells you Who, What, Where, When and Why

After the introduction, the main bit of text gives the reader some <u>details</u> about the story.

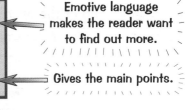

Nathan and his team were trying to figure out who, what, where, when and why.

e.g.

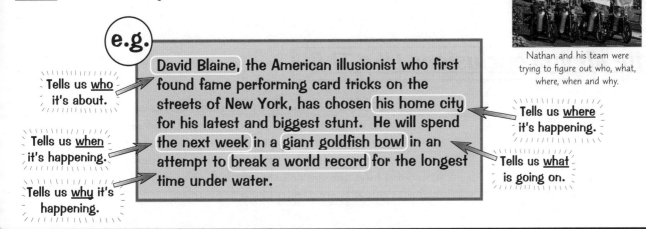

David Blaine, the American illusionist who first found fame performing card tricks on the streets of New York, has chosen his home city for his latest and biggest stunt. He will spend the next week in a giant goldfish bowl in an attempt to break a world record for the longest time under water.

Tells us <u>who</u> it's about.

Tells us <u>when</u> it's happening.

Tells us <u>why</u> it's happening.

Tells us <u>where</u> it's happening.

Tells us <u>what</u> is going on.

Who? What? Where? Nurse, the pills...

This is all fairly obvious really — the introduction gives a general idea of what's in the article, then you get the details. The next page shows you how these details are structured in the main text, before it's all nicely summed up in the conclusion. And they all lived happily ever after...

Structure

The middle of the article gives more details about the points described in the introduction. Then the conclusion sums everything up and leaves the reader with something to think about.

The Body of the text is usually Structured in Paragraphs

Here's one common way of structuring an article:

1) The main points of the text are first given very briefly in the introduction.

2) Each paragraph of the main body of the text then expands on these ideas in turn.

Here's the main body of the whale article from the previous page:

First paragraph expands on first idea in introduction.

Second paragraph expands on second idea in introduction.

> The whale, identified as a humpback that would normally be found in transatlantic waters, is bleeding from a wound to its side. It has been swimming alongside the Houses of Parliament all afternoon, having first been spotted by a French tourist who was walking nearby.
>
> The number of onlookers has rapidly increased during the afternoon as news of Fred's sighting spread through the cafes, shops and offices of Central London. The crowd has been very considerate of the whale's welfare by maintaining a quiet presence.

Conclusions summarise the Main Points

1) Conclusions give a summary of the main points of an article.

2) To be effective, they should leave the reader thinking about the subject of the article.

This summarises what was in the text.

This makes the reader think about their own attitudes.

> The questions that remain unanswered are how Fred came to be in the Thames and whether or not he will live. However, the most intriguing question is why are we, as humans, so interested in his plight?

Write about conclusions Like This

Show that you understand why the conclusion is there.

Show how the conclusion helps the reader to engage with the text.

> The conclusion sums up the main points of the article, such as the concerns about whether the whale will survive or not. This emphasises the main points for the reader. In addition, the last sentence, which asks why humans are so interested, encourages the reader to think more deeply about the subject.

And in conclusion, this is all dead easy...

So let me get this straight — the introduction's at the start and the conclusion's at the end, you say? You're absolutely sure about that then? Well, it's crazy, but it just might work...

List Questions

This section contains lots of advice about how to approach exam questions. You'll need a lasso, a tranquilliser dart and a pick-up truck...

Question 1 usually asks you to List Information

1) The first question in this exam usually asks you to pick out information from a text and write it in a list. Here's an example:

> **Look at the magazine article 'Breakfast with the Queen'.**
> 1. List **ten** things you learn about the way that the Queen of Gondaland eats breakfast.
> [*10 marks*]

2) This type of question is fairly straightforward — but you need to make sure you find enough suitable details to get top marks.

3) The question usually asks you to find 10 things — one for each mark.

It's important to Read the text Carefully

1) After you've read the question, look through the text (some questions tell you to only look at certain paragraphs).

2) As you read, underline points that answer the question. Here's an example:

> The Queen has breakfast at 7.30 am. According to her former butler, she usually has her breakfast on a silver tray in bed. She reads the newspapers during breakfast, and listens to the 'Today' programme on Radio 4.
> Friends say that she likes to have a simple meal of toast and marmalade. Her preferred drink is Earl Grey tea, and she likes this to be in a china cup.
> The Queen often gives her dogs some tidbits of toast. She prefers not to eat the crusts. She usually finishes her breakfast about 8 am.

You can write your Answer in a Numbered List

1) For this type of question, it's a good idea to write your answer as a list, with bullet points or numbered points. Here's an example: ⟶

2) Using numbered points helps you make sure you've listed enough details.

For all the other questions in this exam, you have to write in normal paragraphs.

> 1) Starts breakfast at 7.30 am
> 2) Breakfast on silver tray
> 3) Eats breakfast in bed
> 4) Reads the newspapers
> 5) Listens to Radio 4
> 6) Eats toast and marmalade
> 7) Drinks Earl Grey tea
> 8) Gives dogs toast
> 9) Doesn't like eating crusts
> 10) Finishes breakfast about 8 am

Don't be tired and list-less....

"List" questions are nice and straightforward. So don't waste the opportunity to get some marks — make sure you list enough suitable details, and make sure they're from the right part of the text.

P.E.E.

P.E.E. is a technique that helps you develop points in your answer. It's useful for the <u>trickier exam questions</u> that ask you to say how writers have influenced their readers.

P.E.E. stands for Point Example Explanation

P.E.E. helps you <u>structure</u> your answers to those trickier questions:

1) Make a <u>point</u> to answer the question you've been given.
2) Then give an <u>example</u> from the text (either a quote or a description).
3) After that, <u>explain</u> how your example backs up your point.

Dave tried to cool down his Potentially Explosive Elephant so he could use him in more exam answer

Here's a paragraph from an answer that includes those <u>three</u> things:

This is your point.

This is your example.

This bit is your explanation.

> The writer feels quite angry about school dinners. She says school food is "pallid, tasteless pap". The word "pap" has a disgusted sound to it, showing her opinion about the low quality of the food.

Explain what your example Shows about the Text

1) Your example will usually be a <u>quote</u>, but it can also be a <u>reference</u>, e.g. a description of the pictures, font, layout or structure of the text.
2) The <u>explanation</u> part is very important. It's your chance to make your point <u>clear</u>.

Here are some answers with <u>different types of examples</u> and clear <u>explanations</u>:

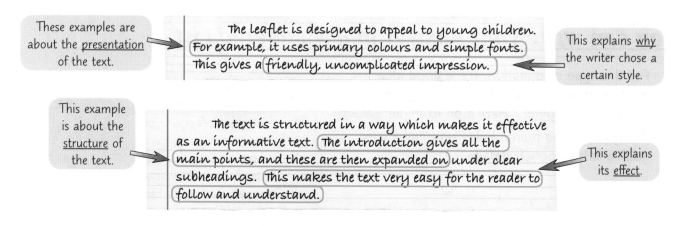

These examples are about the <u>presentation</u> of the text.

> The leaflet is designed to appeal to young children. For example, it uses primary colours and simple fonts. This gives a friendly, uncomplicated impression.

This explains <u>why</u> the writer chose a certain style.

This example is about the <u>structure</u> of the text.

> The text is structured in a way which makes it effective as an informative text. The introduction gives all the main points, and these are then expanded on under clear subheadings. This makes the text very easy for the reader to follow and understand.

This explains its <u>effect</u>.

Would you like to share the joke with the rest of the class?

You don't need to use **P.E.E.** for the simpler exam questions — e.g. if you're asked to list ten facts, then just do that. But **P.E.E.** is really useful for the trickier questions that ask you to discuss writers' techniques. (And remember to have a sly giggle or two over the word **P.E.E.**)

Writing in Paragraphs

You need to know <u>why</u> paragraphs are so important and how to <u>start</u> a good one.

Paragraphs are useful for Structuring your Answers

1) For "list" questions (see p. 27), you can write a list of numbered points. For <u>all the other exam questions</u>, you need to <u>organise</u> your points clearly and <u>link</u> them together — and the best way to do that is to write in <u>paragraphs</u>.

2) If a question's got <u>bullet points</u>, write at least <u>one paragraph</u> for each bullet point.

3) If there are <u>no</u> bullet points in the question, use a <u>paragraph</u> for each main point in your answer.

If you forget to write in paragraphs, you'll feel this silly.

How you Start each New Paragraph is important

<u>Linking</u> your paragraphs together smoothly is an important skill — it makes your writing look <u>more confident</u> and <u>better thought out</u>.

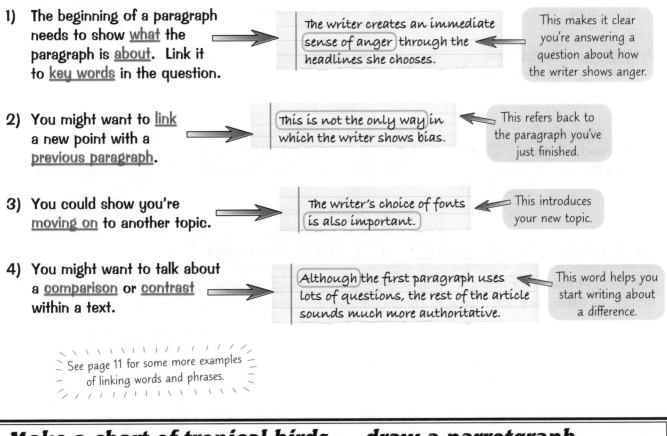

1) The beginning of a paragraph needs to show <u>what</u> the paragraph is <u>about</u>. Link it to <u>key words</u> in the question.

The writer creates an immediate sense of anger through the headlines she chooses.

This makes it clear you're answering a question about how the writer shows anger.

2) You might want to <u>link</u> a new point with a <u>previous paragraph</u>.

This is not the only way in which the writer shows bias.

This refers back to the paragraph you've just finished.

3) You could show you're <u>moving on</u> to another topic.

The writer's choice of fonts is also important.

This introduces your new topic.

4) You might want to talk about a <u>comparison</u> or <u>contrast</u> within a text.

Although the first paragraph uses lots of questions, the rest of the article sounds much more authoritative.

This word helps you start writing about a difference.

See page 11 for some more examples of linking words and phrases.

Make a chart of tropical birds — draw a parrotgraph...

This stuff kind of comes naturally when you've had enough practice. So keep doing practice exams and answering practice questions — pretty soon you'll be producing beautiful answers.

Reading with Insight

"Insight" means noticing the less obvious things about a text.

Think about the writer's Attitude and Motivation

1) You can show insight if you work out what a writer's attitude is (how they feel about the topic). For example:

> There is a strong sense that the writer feels angry about the changes.

2) You could comment on how the writer tries to make readers feel. For example:

> The writer seems to want to make readers feel guilty.

3) You might write about why you think a piece was written. For example:

> Perhaps the writer felt he needed to make sure the memory of his friend was kept alive.

You need to look Beyond what's Obvious

Writers don't always make things obvious. You can use evidence in the text to work out what the writer really means. Make sure you use details from the text though. Don't just guess.

1) Language gives you clues.

> The writer uses words like "endless" and "glum". This implies that he did not enjoy the film.

This phrase is useful for showing you've thought about what the writer really thinks.

2) Pictures with the text might give you some ideas.

> The article appears to be critical of the circus because it includes pictures of animals cramped in cages and fields full of litter.

3) The content of the text will give you hints.

> The writer gives the impression of being in favour of the exam system because she only uses examples of successful candidates.

The Examiner wants to hear Your Opinion

You can get marks for giving a thoughtful personal response. Make sure you focus on the text though — examiners don't want to know your general opinions on various unrelated issues.

THIS WOULD BE GOOD:

> I think the article would remind older people of happier times because it includes so many descriptive details.

THIS WOULD BE BAD:

> I think old people are quite boring.

Make sure you're reading with insight of a cup of tea...

There's lots of really good advice on this page. I'd read it over one more time if I were you. Using some of these higher-level techniques will help you to achieve a 'C' grade in the exam.

Comparing Texts

In the exam, there's usually a question that asks you about <u>both texts</u>. You might have to <u>compare</u> what the writers <u>say</u>, or what they <u>think</u> about something in particular. These questions can be tricky — so here's a page of hints about how to tackle them...

Quickly Plan <u>your answer</u> Before <u>you start</u> Writing

Here's a <u>question</u> that asks you to compare two texts:

> 4. Compare and contrast *Teen Times* and *Youth Out of Control*, using these headings:
>   *   the intended audience of each text;
>   *   the presentation of each text;
>   *   what the texts say about young people.

And here's how you could quickly <u>plan</u> an answer to that question:

Set your notes out in lists, side by side, to help you compare.

Each line of notes matches a bullet point in the question.

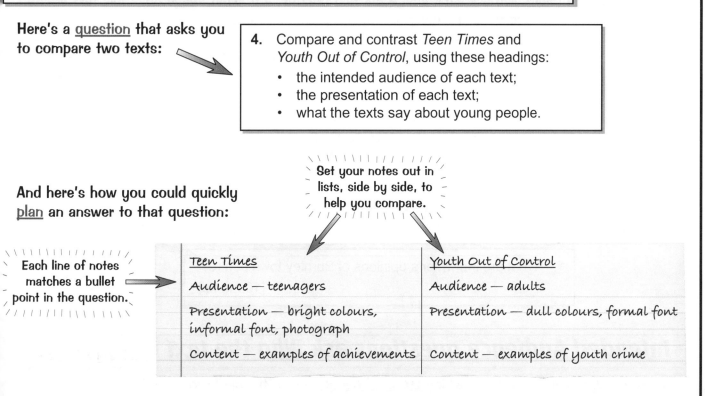

Teen Times	Youth Out of Control
Audience — teenagers	Audience — adults
Presentation — bright colours, informal font, photograph	Presentation — dull colours, formal font
Content — examples of achievements	Content — examples of youth crime

Write an <u>Equal Amount</u> about <u>Each Text</u>

Here's part of a <u>possible answer</u> to the question above:

If the question says 'using these headings', make sure you write your answer under each of the headings.

This paragraph compares the texts directly.

This introduces a difference.

> <u>Presentation</u>
>   The presentation of 'Teen Times' is fun and informal. For example, the headline and subheadings are in brightly-coloured text boxes. This creates a light-hearted tone. In contrast, the presentation of 'Youth Out of Control' is quite formal. For example, it uses a dark grey text box to highlight the advice centre information. This creates a more serious tone.

Next up, all the way from Bolton — oh you said "compare"...

Questions about two texts will sometimes give you some bullet points for guidance. Make sure you cover all of these bullet points in your answer — otherwise you'll lose out on marks.

Other Question Types

Just when you thought it was all over, along I come with yet more question types. Sigh.

You could be asked what Impression a text gives you

1) You could be asked to explain what impression you get of the writer or the things they've written about, e.g. the writer is very happy, the text is about a very successful company.
2) The question might also ask what image the text creates, e.g. what image does this text create of the writer? This is the same thing as the impression it creates.

> Think about what you've learnt about Bob Brown from the text.

> **1.** What impression do you get of the writer, Bob Brown? [10 marks]

Viewpoint/Attitude questions ask what the Writer Thinks

1) You might be asked to work out what a writer's attitude, opinions, viewpoint or thoughts and feelings on a subject are.
2) For any of these you basically just have to pick out what the writer thinks, e.g. the writer's opinion of the car is that it is ugly.

> **1.** What are the writer's opinions of Burnley town centre? [10 marks]

> You only need to write about his opinion of Burnley town centre — don't write about what he thinks of anything else.

Intended Audience questions ask Who the text is Aimed at

1) You might have to work out which group of people the writer wants to read their text, e.g. children, dog owners or teachers (see p.2 for more on audience).
2) You'll usually need to explain your reasons for saying who the text is aimed at as well.

> Write about how each of these things show who the text is aimed at.

> **1.** Who is the leaflet aimed at? Think about:
> - what it says;
> - how it says it. [10 marks]

> You could also be asked about things like how the text is organised or the use of presentational features.

You could also be asked to Analyse Persuasive Techniques

1) Some questions ask you to spot the techniques that writers use to keep readers interested, to argue a point or to persuade them to do something.
2) Sometimes you'll be given bullet points that tell you what to write about for these questions. If you aren't, you should always think about what the text says, how it says it, how the text is organised and how the article has been presented.

> **1.** How does the writer try to encourage you to visit Italy? [10 marks]

> You need to pick out specific techniques like language and the pictures that have been used.

I have a question — can I stop revising now?

Sadly, I'm afraid the answer to that one is 'no'. But on the plus side, you're now into the exam section of the book, where you get to practise some sample exam questions. Woop woop.

Summary of the Exam

I bet you're just aching to know all about your exams. Well, the next two pages tell you what the examiners have got in store for you and give you some tips on how to keep them happy.

Each Exam Lasts for One Hour

1) Whether you're doing GCSE English Language or GCSE English, you have to do two exams.

2) They're the same exams for both courses, and they cover Unit 1: Reading: non-fiction texts and Unit 2: Writing: information and ideas.

3) You get one hour for each exam.

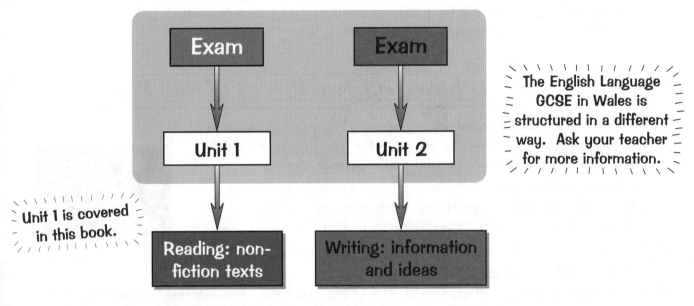

The English Language GCSE in Wales is structured in a different way. Ask your teacher for more information.

Unit 1 is covered in this book.

The Front Page tells you What To Do

First up — what to do when you plonk yourself down in that nice, comfy exam chair (there's more on the structure of the Unit 1 exam on the next page):

1) The front page of the question paper will tell you what you should have in front of you. Read it through and make sure you've got everything. Here's what you should have for the Unit 1 exam:

   • A question paper which will have all the questions and one of the non-fiction texts you'll be asked about.

   • A separate booklet (called the Resource Material) containing the other non-fiction text.

   • A 12-page answer book to write your answers in.

2) Make sure you fill in all the details you're asked for on the front of the answer book, or you won't get any marks at all — not ideal.

3) Make sure you've got the foundation tier paper, not the higher one.

4) Read all the instructions on the front page of the question paper to remind you what to do.

My mum tells me what to do...

So there you are, just two exams for your GCSE in English or English Language. There are controlled assessments to do for Unit 3 and Unit 4 as well, but they're for another day — all we're looking at in this book is Unit 1. It's the most fun bit anyway, at least, that's what I think.

Summary of the Exam

This page is about the different <u>questions</u> on the Unit 1 exam, and how many <u>marks</u> each one's worth. Crikey, with all this info to take in about the exam, they'll be giving you an exam on the exam next...

The <u>Unit 1 exam is worth</u> 40 Marks

1) The whole exam is worth <u>40 marks</u>, and counts for <u>20%</u> of your total GCSE mark (for either GCSE English Language or GCSE English).

2) The questions are most often worth <u>10 marks each</u>, so the exam is likely to have <u>four 10 mark questions</u>.

3) Sometimes though, there will be questions worth <u>5 marks</u>, or a question might be broken down into parts that are worth <u>1, 2 or 3 marks</u>.

The <u>Unit 1 exam is based on</u> Two Pieces <u>of</u> Non-Fiction Text

1) The Unit 1 exam will be based on <u>two pieces of non-fiction text</u> that you haven't seen before — one will be in the <u>question paper</u> and the other will be in the <u>separate booklet</u> you're given in the exam.

2) The texts you'll be given could be anything from <u>leaflets</u>, <u>letters</u>, <u>reports</u>, <u>biographies</u>, <u>articles</u> (from <u>newspapers</u>, <u>magazines</u>, <u>brochures</u> or the <u>internet</u>), <u>advertisements</u> or <u>fact sheets</u>.

In his exam, James was faced with a type of text he had never seen before.

3) For one of the questions you'll have to <u>compare</u> the two texts — this will usually be the <u>last question</u>.

4) All the other questions will each be on <u>one</u> of the two texts. For example, if there are four questions the first two could be on the <u>first text</u>, the third question could be on the <u>other text</u> and the final question could be on <u>both</u>.

5) Make sure you read the questions properly (you'll be told which text you should write about) so that your answer is about the <u>right text or texts</u>.

<u>Answer</u> All the Questions

1) You have to answer <u>every question</u> in the Unit 1 exam.

2) You have <u>one hour</u> for this exam — that <u>includes</u> the time you'll spend <u>reading</u> the texts you've been given.

> You should spend a total of about <u>7-8 minutes reading</u> <u>each text</u> and about <u>45 minutes writing your answers</u>.

3) You should spend about <u>11 minutes</u> answering the <u>10 mark questions</u>, and <u>5-6 minutes</u> on any <u>5 mark questions</u>. If there are any questions worth <u>1, 2 or 3 marks</u> only spend <u>a minute or two</u> answering them.

4) In general, the <u>more marks</u> a question is worth, the <u>longer</u> you should spend on it.

That's the theory sorted — turn over to see an exam...

Now you know how the exam is structured, I bet you're dying to have a look at an actual paper. Well, I was feeling nice today so I made one just for you — take a look at the next few pages.

Exam Paper — Questions

Here are some lovely **example questions** to get you in the mood for all that exam fun.
The texts for these questions are printed on the next two pages.

The **Resource Material** is from a website brochure produced by Roo,
an Australian themed restaurant.

The other item is a newspaper article entitled 'Raving about Roo' by Ruby Jones.

Look at the website brochure for Roo, on the next page.

1. List **ten** types of food and drink mentioned in the website brochure that
    are available at Roo.

    [10 marks]

    Putting your points in a numbered list will help you check that you've written enough points.

2. How does the website brochure try to persuade readers that Roo is a
    good place to eat for both adults and children?

    [10 marks]

    Make sure you write about both age groups.

Now look at the newspaper article by Ruby Jones ('Raving about Roo').

3. What are the author's thoughts and feelings about Roo?

    You should include:
    *   what she liked;
    *   what she did not like;
    *   her overall impression.

    Don't miss out any of the bullet points.

    [10 marks]

**You should now use details and information <u>from both texts</u> to answer the
following question:**

4. Both of these texts are about the restaurant, Roo. Compare and contrast
    them, using the following headings:

    This means you need to write about the similarities and differences between the two texts.

    *   how the restaurant looks;
    *   the service at Roo;
    *   the prices at Roo.

    [10 marks]

"How did you find the exam?" "It was just on the table..."

Some exam questions come up time after time: list 10 things you learn, what are the writer's thoughts
and feelings, compare and contrast the two texts... There shouldn't be any big surprises in the exam.

Exam Text: Website Brochure

Here's one of the texts for the exam questions — it's a web page for the restaurant, Roo.

© iStockphoto.com/Francisco Romero

ROO

BOOK ONLINE

CONTACT US

FIND US

MENUS

- LUNCHTIME MENU
- EVENING MENU
- CHILDREN'S MENU
- SEASONAL SPECIALS

GALLERY

KIDS' CORNER!

Our special children's menu, available in the family restaurant, features child-sized portions with miniature prices! Kids can tuck into a wide range of scrummy dishes, ranging from kangaroo burgers for the more adventurous through to plainer pizza and pasta dishes for those who prefer to play it safe.

Welcome to Roo, Liverpool's exotic new eaterie!

Roo is located in a lovingly renovated former warehouse right next to the river. It's kept some of the traditional features of the original warehouse but given them a contemporary twist. For example, some of the old machines have been given a new lease of life as our decorations and we've also created huge, ceiling-high windows in the old brick walls — so you'll have an amazing view wherever you sit. The restaurant is arranged over two floors, with family dining on the ground floor and adults only on the first floor.

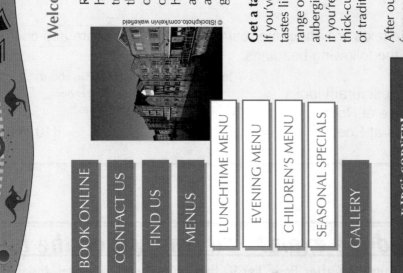
© iStockphoto.com/kelvin wakefield

Get a taste of Australia

If you've always wondered what kangaroo, emu or shark tastes like, this is the place for you. We also offer a wide range of mouth-watering vegetarian dishes, from stuffed aubergines to our speciality roasted vegetable frittata. But if you're simply after a plate of freshly-caught plaice and thick-cut chips, our family restaurant serves a wide range of traditional favourites.

After our customers told us that they just couldn't choose from our wide range of delicious Australian dishes, we came up with a solution — a special "Taster Menu" that lets you sample shark, ostrich and kangaroo, all for less than £20! And for those of you with a sweet tooth, we have an assortment of delicious desserts — our peach pavlova is particularly popular.

Service with a smile

Our friendly, smartly-dressed and professional staff are happy to help, and we pride ourselves on our quick service. If you want to know a bit more about the food you're eating, don't hesitate to ask.

A tranquil haven

Roo is the perfect place for a romantic meal. Our upper floor is exclusively for adults, so you're guaranteed peace and quiet, as well as stunning views of the river. Our adult-only restaurant with its private alcoves, soft candlelight and designer decor will give you an intimate, relaxing, romantic experience.

We welcome families too in our friendly family restaurant. For our younger visitors we supply goody bags with crayons and kangaroo stickers to keep them entertained until their food arrives. We also provide high chairs and clean, spacious baby-changing facilities.

FOODIE FRIDAYS

Are you keen to broaden your culinary horizons? Then our Foodie Fridays are for you! Comfortably seated at tables surrounding our glass-walled kitchen, you'll be able to see exactly what the chef is doing as he prepares your meal. When you've finished eating, you'll be given a folder containing all of the evening's recipes to take home.

Delicious drinks for every taste

We're very proud of our selection of fine wines (starting at £14 a bottle), and our knowledgeable waiters will help you select the perfect wine to complement your meal. If you're the designated driver (or under 18), try our range of sparkling soft drinks, fruit juices and smoothies. We also offer delicious milkshakes in our family restaurant.

© iStockphoto.com/Michael Maeyer

A couple enjoying our unique atmosphere.

Exam Text: Newspaper Article

Here's the other text for the exam on page 35. This one's a newspaper review of the restaurant.

Raving about Roo

Ruby Jones visits Liverpool's newest restaurant, and can't stop talking about it.

Last night was a night of totally new experiences as I sampled the delights of Roo, Liverpool's most exciting new restaurant. Roo is owned and run by an Australian couple, who have attempted (and, in my opinion, succeeded) to bring a taste of the unfamiliar cuisines of far-flung countries to Liverpool's diners. They certainly offer some exciting dishes — ostrich, shark, crocodile and kangaroo were just a few of the options on the menu.

The restaurant has a superb riverside location and is housed in a converted warehouse, with huge windows giving views up and down the Mersey. The interior looks fantastic — the high ceilings make it feel light and spacious, and some of the original warehouse equipment (winches, pulleys etc.) are displayed to great effect. However, on the adults-only floor, comfort has been sacrificed a little for the sake of trendiness — a few cushions would have made an evening on the designer stainless steel seats much more enjoyable! The opposite seemed to be true of the 'family restaurant' downstairs, where cushioned booths and bean-bags are the order of the day — comfortable certainly, but more in keeping with an American diner than a former warehouse.

Roo offers a 'Taster Menu', for people who are curious to try some unusual dishes, but don't necessarily want a whole helping of something they might not like. A taster menu main course is £19 per person (not including drinks), or for £30 you can add a starter and dessert. Having heard great things about Roo's desserts, we both opted for the three course meal — a pricey choice, but on the whole, well worth the money. We had it with a bottle of (well-priced) Australian white wine and two bottles of mineral water and it came to £80 overall.

We started with crocodile goujons. They tasted like a strange (but not unpleasant) cross between meat and fish. They were served with a sweet chilli dip and a side salad, which were also very enjoyable, and left me eager for my main course.

The goujons were followed by a grilled meat platter — ostrich steak, shark fillet and kangaroo steak, served with new potatoes and seasonal vegetables. The ostrich was a little chewy for my liking, but as I don't know how it should be cooked, it could have been down to the nature of the meat rather than the quality of the cooking. The shark fillet was pleasant, and it had been cooked in a delicious lemon and garlic sauce. But the real highlight of the meal was the kangaroo steak, which was wonderfully tender and had a delicious flavour, something like prime beef but stronger.

The dessert was the most disappointing part of the evening — a fairly run-of-the-mill fruit salad (though using exotic fruits such as star fruit, guava and dragon fruit). It was perfectly pleasant, it was just a bit of a let-down compared to the other two courses, and it definitely wasn't worth the price tag of £8.50 (if bought separately, rather than as part of a three course meal).

The service, for the most part, was good. Our waitress was friendly, and took the time to explain each dish as she brought it over. However, her white apron collected a few food stains over the course of the evening, which gave the impression that hygiene wasn't a priority. As the restaurant grew busier, it also became a lot harder to attract her attention. I've heard some mixed reviews of the service at Roo — a friend of mine ate here and complained that she waited nearly an hour for her main course, and that the staff seemed to know very little about the food. This is a far cry from my experience, so it looks like the staff at Roo have pulled their socks up, although there's still a bit of work to do.

Dividing the restaurant into a 'family' section and a 'grown-up' section is a great idea. The only problem is that it's still quite noisy — chatter from the family restaurant on the ground floor drifts upwards, making it a little hard to have a quiet conversation.

All in all, the evening was a success. I'd definitely recommend Roo for people who are looking for something a bit different, or for families who want good food in a child-friendly environment. The food was delicious (although a little pricey) and I'd definitely go back with friends. However, due to the noise and the rather uncomfortable seating, it's probably not somewhere I'd choose for a romantic evening.

Mark Scheme

Ever thought, "If only I could get inside that examiner's head"? Not literally of course — that would be hideous. But these pages will show you just how they'd mark the exam on page 35 — so that you know exactly what to do to get marks. Ooh, isn't it exciting...

How they work out your Grade

Mark the four questions individually using the mark schemes on pages 38-41.
Then add up the four marks and use the table below to get your mock Unit 1 grade.
(This is just a general guide — the grade boundaries vary from year to year.)

Marks	8-11	12-15	16-19	20-23	24-40
Grade	G	F	E	D	C

If you're taking your exams in Wales, the marks available for each question might be different.

Of course, your final GCSE English Language or GCSE English grade is an average of this, your Unit 2 exam and your controlled assessments. But the grade you get for this exam shows the grade you're on course for.

Question 1

> 1. List **ten** types of food and drink mentioned in the website brochure that are available at Roo.
>
> [10 marks]

Here are some possible Points for an Answer

1) In the first question, the examiners usually let you score some easy marks. All you need to do is write down a load of points in a big old list.

2) This type of question checks that you've understood what you've read, and that you can pick out the bits from the text that answer the question.

3) You can score up to 10 marks on this question, so you should try and write ten different points.

Here are some points you could include, but these aren't the only possibilities — if you found a valid point that isn't here, you'd still get a mark for it.

• kangaroo burgers	• plaice
• emu	• thick-cut chips
• shark	• peach pavlova
• ostrich	• fine wines
• pizza	• sparkling soft drinks
• pasta dishes	• fruit juices
• stuffed aubergines	• smoothies
• vegetable frittata	• milkshakes

Mark Scheme

Question 2

2. How does the website brochure try to persuade readers that Roo is a good place to eat for both adults and children?

[10 marks]

Here are some possible Points for an Answer

The examiners are looking for <u>how</u> the website brochure persuades you, not just <u>what</u> it says or does. Here are some points you could make — but remember, these are <u>just suggestions</u>.

<u>Adults</u>:
- The "exotic" menu, including emu, shark and kangaroo, suggests an out-of-the-ordinary dining experience which would appeal to adults looking for new and exciting things to eat.
- The photo of a happy couple in evening clothes hints at a romantic atmosphere, which makes it appeal to adults who want a more intimate experience.
- Interesting adjectives, such as "private", "soft" and "designer" also make the restaurant seem intimate and romantic, which would appeal to adults.

<u>Children</u>:
- Plainer foods, such as "pizza and pasta", are available to appeal to children who often prefer more simple options than adults. There are also "child-sized portions" of things like kangaroo burgers to appeal to "more adventurous" children.
- The brochure uses persuasive adjectives, such as "special" to describe the children's menu and "scrummy" to describe the dishes. This makes the reader think that children are specially catered for in the restaurant.
- The photo on the right hand side shows a child enjoying her meal and sitting in a comfy chair, so it is clear that the restaurant is a good place for children.

Here's a Marking Grid for question 2

Mark	Quality of Answer
0 marks	Nothing written that helps to answer the question.
1 mark	One or two simple points that attempt to answer the question.
2-4 marks	A few simple points that spot, but don't explain, the persuasive techniques used. Large chunks of the text may be copied out as evidence.
5-7 marks	Makes some points that explain why the website is persuasive, backed up with appropriate examples from the text. Covers both parts of the question (adults and children).
8-10 marks	Makes several valid points that clearly explain how different features of the website are persuasive, using relevant examples from the text. Both parts are covered in detail.

Mark Scheme

Question 3

> 3. What are the author's thoughts and feelings about Roo?
> You should include:
> * what she liked;
> * what she did not like;
> * her overall impression.   **[10 marks]**

Here are some possible Points for an Answer

For this type of question, you need to gather information from different parts of the article. Here are some of the points you might include.

What she liked:

* Ruby Jones liked the location of the restaurant and the decorations. This is clear as she uses positive language to describe them, such as "superb riverside location" and "fantastic" interior.
* She liked some of the food, in particular the kangaroo steak, which she describes as the "highlight" of the meal. She says it was "wonderfully tender and had a delicious flavour".

What she did not like:

* She wasn't very impressed with the "designer stainless steel seats". She says "comfort has been sacrificed a little for the sake of trendiness" which shows that she thought the chairs were fashionable, but very uncomfortable to sit on.
* Even though she says it was "perfectly pleasant", it's obvious Ruby Jones was disappointed with the dessert she had as she describes it as "a bit of a let-down". The negative words she uses, such as "run-of-the-mill", highlight her disappointment.

Her overall impression:

* Her overall impression is positive as she says "All in all, the evening was a success". She thinks the food was "delicious" even though it was "pricey", but she'd "definitely go back".

Here's a Marking Grid for question 3

Mark	Quality of Answer
0 marks	Nothing written that helps to answer the question.
1 mark	One or two simple points that attempt to answer the question.
2-4 marks	A few simple points that spot some of the things she did and didn't like. Large chunks of the text may be copied out as evidence.
5-7 marks	Makes some points that pick out the writer's thoughts and feelings about the restaurant, backed up with examples from the text. Covers all three bullet points.
8-10 marks	Makes several valid points that clearly identify and attempt to explain the writer's thoughts and feelings, using relevant examples from the article. All three bullet points are covered in detail.

Mark Scheme

Question 4

4. Both of these texts are about the restaurant, Roo. Compare and contrast them, using the following headings:
   - how the restaurant looks;
   - the service at Roo;
   - the prices at Roo. [10 marks]

Here are some possible Points for an Answer

You're being tested on how well you can select the right material and make comparisons. The question gives you help in organising your answer, so make sure you follow their headings.

How the restaurant looks:
- The website brochure says the restaurant is decorated with the "old machines" from the warehouse that have been given a "new lease of life". The newspaper article also says that "the original warehouse equipment" is displayed "to great effect". The brochure only says good things about how the restaurant looks, but the article says some of the features make the ground floor look more like "an American diner than a former warehouse".

The service at Roo:
- The website brochure describes its staff as "friendly, smartly-dressed and professional" and says they are "happy to help". The newspaper article generally agrees with this, saying "The service, for the most part, was good", and compliments the "friendly" waitress. They both make the service sound good, but Ruby Jones mentions that someone she knows "waited nearly an hour" for her food and thought the staff didn't know very much.

The prices at Roo:
- The website brochure shows that the restaurant is an affordable place to eat, saying the taster menu is "less than £20" and the children's meals have "miniature prices". Ruby Jones doesn't really agree with this. She says it was "pricey" but does go on to say it was "well worth the money".

Here's a Marking Grid for question 4

Mark	Quality of Answer
0 marks	Nothing written that helps to answer the question.
1 mark	One or two simple points that attempt to answer the question.
2-4 marks	A few simple points with little and poorly chosen evidence from the texts. May not cover all three bullet points or may only talk about one text.
5-7 marks	Makes some points that compare the website and the newspaper article, backed up with examples from both texts. Covers all three bullet points and talks about both texts.
8-10 marks	Makes several valid points that clearly compare the two texts, using relevant examples from them both. Covers all three bullet points and both texts in detail.

Grade E & D Answers to Question 1

These two pages show you <u>example answers</u> to <u>question 1</u> of the exam on page 35, starting with an <u>"E" grade answer</u> and working up to a <u>"C" grade answer</u>.

For question 1 you have to <u>Find Information</u>

1) Have a look at question 1 <u>before</u> reading the first text — that way you'll know what you're looking for from the start.

2) As you read the text through, <u>circle</u> the types of <u>food</u> and <u>drink</u> that the restaurant serves. Then you can <u>write them down</u> as your answer.

Don't scribble on this book if it belongs to your school — teachers hate that.

Here's an <u>"E" grade</u> answer to question 1.

It would be clearer for the examiner to mark if you followed the question instructions and wrote your answer as a list.

> There are many types of exotic foods and drinks you can get at Roo restaurant. For adults who feel like a drink there is wine (from £14 a bottle) and for children there are delicious things like milkshakes. Some good examples of the types of food you can eat are (ostrich and kangaroo.)

You don't need extra details like this.

These are good examples but you need to give more to get top marks.

There are <u>four</u> different types of food and drink mentioned in this answer, so it would be given <u>four marks</u> out of ten.

You should write your answer as a <u>List</u>

1) If you are asked to "<u>list</u>", then simply <u>write a list</u>. It's not a trick question — it really is that straightforward.

2) This question tests your ability to <u>pick out</u> relevant information, not your writing skills, so keep your answers as <u>simple</u> as possible to <u>save time</u>.

This is a <u>"D" grade</u> answer to the question.

Bullet points are a good way to separate your points, but they don't tell you at a glance how many points you have.

- kangaroo
- shark
- stuffed aubergines
- fine wine
- smoothies
- wine

Some questions need longer answers, but for a list question one or two words will do.

Make sure you don't use the same point more than once — it's easy to do if the information is repeated in the text.

This answer lists five <u>different</u> types of food and drink, so it would get five marks. Remember, the examiner wouldn't ask for 10 points unless there were <u>at least that many</u>. If you haven't found ten different points, have a quick <u>look again</u> at the text to see if you can <u>find some more</u>.

Grade C Answer to Question 1

There's an example "C" grade answer to question 1 on this page. It's more thrilling than cycling blindfolded down the side of a mountain in the middle of winter whilst wearing a silly hat. And I can tell you from experience, that's pretty thrilling.

Make sure you make Ten Points

1) This is one of the nice, straightforward "list" questions. Have a look back at the advice on page 27 and it should be a walk in the park.

2) If you write a numbered list you can easily see if you have enough points.

3) Make sure all your points answer the question though — don't write anything down unless it's a type of food or drink that the website says is served in the restaurant.

4) Make sure your spelling's correct. A lot of your answer will come straight from the text, so there's no excuse for making mistakes.

Here's a "C" grade answer to question 1.

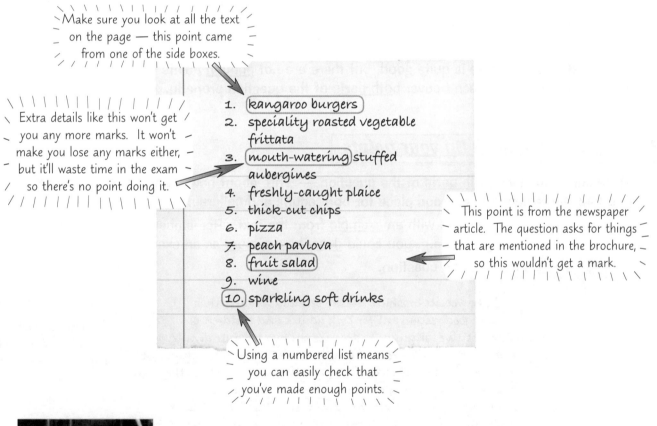

Make sure you look at all the text on the page — this point came from one of the side boxes.

Extra details like this won't get you any more marks. It won't make you lose any marks either, but it'll waste time in the exam so there's no point doing it.

1. kangaroo burgers
2. speciality roasted vegetable frittata
3. mouth-watering stuffed aubergines
4. freshly-caught plaice
5. thick-cut chips
6. pizza
7. peach pavlova
8. fruit salad
9. wine
10. sparkling soft drinks

This point is from the newspaper article. The question asks for things that are mentioned in the brochure, so this wouldn't get a mark.

Using a numbered list means you can easily check that you've made enough points.

With a top speed of 30mph, Hamish was determined not to be made into a burger.

This answer makes nine valid points, so it would get nine marks and put you well on course for a "C" grade. These "list" questions are really worth practising because they're an easy way to get a lot of marks.

Grade E & D Answers to Question 2

Right, that's question 1 done, now lets move on to <u>question 2</u>. Have a look back at pages 35-37 for the exam questions and texts.

This question is about Persuasive Techniques

1)   You need to find the <u>features</u> of the website brochure which <u>persuade</u> you that the restaurant is a good place to eat for children and adults.

2)   Then you need to explain <u>how</u> these features make the page persuasive.

Here's an <u>"E" grade</u> answer to question 2.

> The website brochure explains that there are "exotic" foods such as "kangaroo, emu or shark" for adults and "plainer" foods such as "pizza" and "pasta" for children, which shows that there is something for everyone. The website also tries to persuade readers that it is a good place for both adults and children by explaining that there is family dining on the ground floor and adults only on the first floor. This means that the adults will not be annoyed by children making a noise.

This bit hasn't explained why this makes the restaurant a good place to eat for children.

This bit should explain why adults might like exotic food, and why children might prefer plain food.

This is taken directly from the text so it should be in quotation marks.

Some of what is written here is quite good, but there are not <u>enough</u> points — and one of the points doesn't cover <u>both parts</u> of the question properly.

Use Examples to Back Up your points

1)   Make sure you cover <u>both parts</u> of the question — write about how the website persuades you that the restaurant is a good place for both <u>adults</u> and <u>children</u>.

2)   <u>Back up</u> each point you make with an <u>example</u> from the text. Remember though — not all examples have to be <u>quotes</u>, e.g. you could <u>describe a picture</u> as an example.

This is a <u>"D" grade</u> answer to the question.

> The website brochure tries to persuade readers that Roo is a good restaurant for both adults and children by using positive language to describe the two separate dining areas. In the family restaurant there are "high chairs and clean, spacious baby-changing facilities", which makes the restaurant sound very child friendly. On the adults only floor there are "private alcoves" and there is "soft candlelight", which makes it sound like the restaurant is a "romantic experience", so it would appeal to adults.
>
> The website brochure also mentions different kinds of drinks to interest people of all ages. There are milkshakes and smoothies for children and a "selection of fine wines" for adults. The pictures are persuasive too as there is one of adults and one of a child.

This is a good explanation of how the language is persuasive.

Covers both parts of the question all the way through.

This is too vague — it needs to explain why the pictures are persuasive.

This answer starts out really well by <u>explaining</u> why the website appeals to <u>both</u> adults and children. At the end though, it starts to just <u>spot</u> features without explaining how they persuade.

Grade C Answer to Question 2

When you're answering exam questions, try and remember to K.I.S.S. your answer. Or, in other words, "Keep it Simple and Short". Don't go rambling on about things that aren't related to the question, like what you had for dinner last night or what your favourite colour of jelly is.

Use P.E.E. when answering questions like this one

1) For each <u>point</u> you make, find an <u>example</u> to back it up, then <u>explain</u> how this makes the website brochure <u>persuasive</u>.

2) Make sure your answer is <u>balanced</u> — make roughly the <u>same number</u> of points for why the restaurant is a good place for <u>adults</u>, and for why it's a good place for <u>children</u>.

3) Try and use your <u>own words</u> instead of just copying big chunks of the text — this shows you've <u>thought about</u> what you're writing.

Here's a <u>"C" grade</u> answer to question 2.

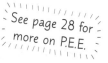
See page 28 for more on P.E.E.

> The website brochure persuades readers that Roo is a good place to eat for both adults and children by describing how the restaurant is divided into two zones "with family dining on the ground floor and adults only on the first floor". This shows that families can make lots of noise and enjoy themselves without upsetting anyone, and adults can have a quieter, more relaxed dinner if they want to.
>
> In the family zone there are child-friendly features such as "high chairs" and "baby-changing facilities", which persuades parents that the restaurant is well-equipped for young children. Children are also given "goody bags" to keep them occupied until the food arrives. This would reassure parents that their children won't get bored.
>
> On the adult floor, the brochure says there is an "intimate, relaxing, romantic" environment. There is also a photograph of a couple enjoying a romantic evening together. These two things combine to show the reader that the restaurant is a great place for adults who want a more relaxed, private dinner.
>
> The menu offers a wide range of both "traditional" and "exotic" dishes for adults, as well as offering "child-sized portions" for children. The adults' menu is described as "mouth-watering" and "delicious", which will appeal to adults wanting an exciting meal out. The brochure uses a childish word, "scrummy", to describe the children's meals, which shows that the restaurant is aimed at children as well as adults.

This point uses P.E.E. — it makes a Point, gives an Example and then Explains how this answers the question.

This is a good way to link points together.

Good use of short quotes worked into the text.

This is a very <u>well-balanced</u> answer. It <u>explains</u> a number of points well and covers how the website appeals to both children and adults <u>equally</u>.

The children's play area was state-of-the-art.

Grade E & D Answers to Question 3

Here are some sample answers to question 3. Enjoy.

Question 3 is asking for the writer's Opinions

1) This question is asking you to give the writer's thoughts and feelings in your own words, using short quotes as evidence.

2) It's a bit different to question 1, as you have to work out what the writer thinks rather than just understanding what she says.

This is an "E" grade answer to question 3.

> The author liked the crocodile goujons as she says they were "enjoyable" but she thought the fruit salad wasn't very good. She also really liked the "superb riverside location". However, she thought the "hygiene" in the restaurant wasn't that good though. Overall she thought the food was "delicious" and she'd "definitely go back" again.

You could also say what she didn't like about how the restaurant looks, e.g. the "cushioned booths and bean-bags".

There's more to say about her overall impression, e.g. the food was a bit "pricey".

This answer makes a few good points, but it needs to explain some of the points a bit better. It also needs much more detail — there are a lot of the writer's thoughts and feelings that haven't been mentioned.

Use the Bullet Points as a Guide

1) The bullet points tell you what you should write about in your answer — so make sure you cover them all.

2) You need to find out what the writer thinks and how she feels about the restaurant. However, it might not say "I liked the restaurant because..." though — you have to work it out yourself from the text.

This is a "D" grade answer to question 3.

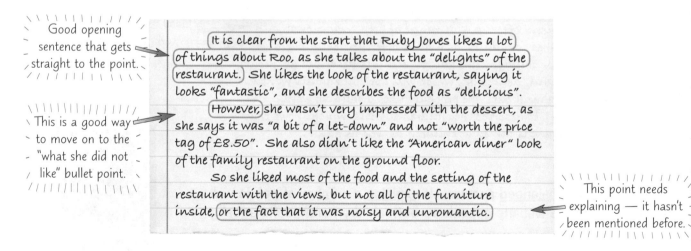

Good opening sentence that gets straight to the point.

This is a good way to move on to the "what she did not like" bullet point.

> It is clear from the start that Ruby Jones likes a lot of things about Roo, as she talks about the "delights" of the restaurant. She likes the look of the restaurant, saying it looks "fantastic", and she describes the food as "delicious".
> However, she wasn't very impressed with the dessert, as she says it was "a bit of a let-down" and not "worth the price tag of £8.50". She also didn't like the "American diner" look of the family restaurant on the ground floor.
> So she liked most of the food and the setting of the restaurant with the views, but not all of the furniture inside, or the fact that it was noisy and unromantic.

This point needs explaining — it hasn't been mentioned before.

This answer covers the first two bullet points well, but doesn't cover 'her overall impression' in enough detail.

Grade C Answer to Question 3

Here's a lovely "C" grade answer to question 3. Aren't I nice. Well, to be honest, it would be nicer if I made you a delicious chocolate cake to take your mind off revision, but unfortunately my oven blew up last week, and cooking things on the radiator isn't very successful.

Cover All Three bullet points Equally

1) For this question, you need to show that you understand what the writer means.

2) Go through the article from start to finish, mentioning each of the writer's thoughts and feelings in turn — make sure you say each time whether it's something she likes or dislikes.

3) You've got to give lots of examples from the text to answer this question — every time you say one of the things that the writer likes or dislikes, make sure you quote the bit of text that shows it. Sometimes, you might also have to explain how the quote shows what the writer thinks.

Here's a "C" grade answer to question 3.

> Ruby Jones obviously likes the restaurant as the first line says she "can't stop talking about it". She's impressed with the "superb riverside location" and with the appearance of the restaurant, describing it as "fantastic" and "light and spacious". However, she does not like the "designer stainless steel seats", as she found them uncomfortable. She also does not particularly like the "cushioned booths and bean-bags" as she feels they are "more in keeping with an American diner than a former warehouse".
>
> She likes almost all of the food she eats, even though she thinks her meal was "a pricey choice". She compliments the "very enjoyable" crocodile goujons, the "wonderfully tender" kangaroo steak, and the "pleasant" shark fillet. There were some parts of the meal she did not like though, such as the "chewy" ostrich and the fruit salad. She highlights her disappointment in the dessert by saying it was "a let-down" and it was "run-of-the-mill".
>
> Jones thinks that separating "family" and "grown-up" dining over two floors is a "great idea" as well, although she still found the adult restaurant a bit "noisy". She thinks this is a "problem", as it made it "hard to have a quiet conversation".
>
> Despite her complaints, Jones's overall impression is positive, as she says she'd "definitely recommend" it and she'd "definitely go back". She thinks the food was "delicious (although a little pricey)" but overall "well worth the money".

Well-chosen examples to back up the point.

This is good — it mentions both a like and a dislike.

This gets straight to the point about her overall impression.

This answer is well-organised and covers most of the writer's thoughts and feelings from the article. It uses quotes really well to back up the points that have been made, and the answer is balanced (all three bullet points have been covered quite well).

The lads reckoned they'd covered all the bullet points pretty well.

Grade E & D Answers to Question 4

Last question now. Remind yourself of the questions and texts by looking back at pages 35-37.

Use the Bullet Points as Subheadings for this question

1) Question 4 <u>tells you</u> what you need to write about. Make sure you write your answer in <u>three parts</u>, using each <u>bullet point</u> as a <u>subheading</u>.

2) Use <u>examples</u> from <u>both texts</u> to back up the points you make in your answer.

This is an <u>"E" grade</u> answer to question 4.

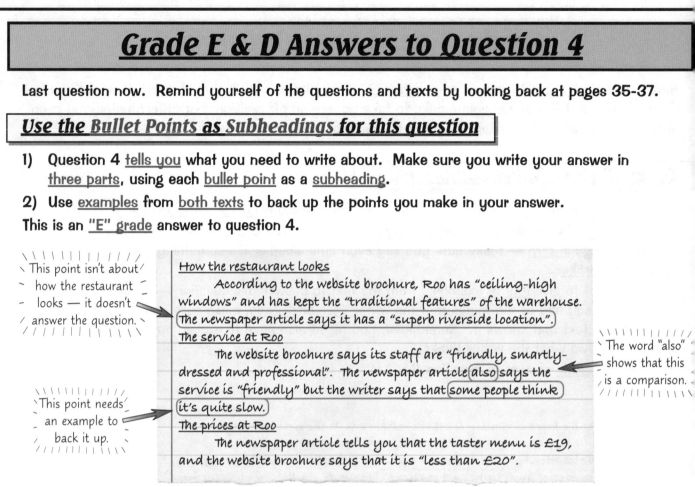

This point isn't about how the restaurant looks — it doesn't answer the question.

This point needs an example to back it up.

How the restaurant looks
    According to the website brochure, Roo has "ceiling-high windows" and has kept the "traditional features" of the warehouse. The newspaper article says it has a "superb riverside location".

The service at Roo
    The website brochure says its staff are "friendly, smartly-dressed and professional". The newspaper article also says the service is "friendly" but the writer says that some people think it's quite slow.

The prices at Roo
    The newspaper article tells you that the taster menu is £19, and the website brochure says that it is "less than £20".

The word "also" shows that this is a comparison.

This answer needs to make more <u>comparisons</u> between the texts, not just <u>statements</u> about what each text says.

Make sure you Compare the texts

1) You have to <u>compare</u> the two texts. Write a point about one of the texts, then use a <u>linking word</u>, e.g. "<u>similarly</u>", "<u>in contrast to</u>", to show how the other text is <u>similar</u> or <u>different</u>.

2) Try and write the <u>same amount</u> about each text.

This is a <u>"D" grade</u> answer to question 4.

How the restaurant looks
    The website brochure describes how the restaurant still has some of the "traditional features" of the old warehouse, but has given them a "contemporary twist" to turn them into decorations. Similarly, the newspaper article mentions that the "original warehouse equipment", is on display "to great effect".

The service at Roo
    Both the website brochure and the newspaper article describe the service as "friendly". However, the writer of the newspaper article also says that it was difficult to get the waitress's attention.

The prices at Roo
    The website brochure mentions cheaper prices than the newspaper article. The brochure says the taster menu is "less than £20" but the newspaper article says that it was £30 for three courses.

Here's a linking word to show that it's a comparison.

This is good — it shows both a similarity and a difference.

There's a lot more detail in the text about this which should be covered here.

This answer makes some <u>good comparisons</u>, but needs to cover the <u>third heading</u> in more <u>detail</u>.